SEMICOLON

SEMICOLON

The Past, Present, and Future
of a Misunderstood Mark

CECELIA WATSON

ecco

An Imprint of HarperCollins Publishers

HarperCollins books may be purchased for educational, business, or sales promotional use. For information, please e-mail the Special Markets Department at SPsales@harpercollins.com.

FIRST EDITION

Designed by Suet Yee Chong
Illustrations by Anthony Russo

Library of Congress Cataloging-in-Publication Data

Names: Watson, Cecelia.
Title: Semicolon : the past, present, and future of a misunderstood mark / Cecelia Watson.
Description: First edition. | New York : Ecco, 2019. | Includes bibliographical references and index.
Identifiers: LCCN 2018045968 (print) | LCCN 2018056939 (ebook) | ISBN 9780062853073 (ebook) | ISBN 9780062853059 | ISBN 9780062853066 | ISBN 9780062917935 | ISBN 9780062917942
Subjects: LCSH: English language—Punctuation. | Semicolon.
Classification: LCC PE1450 (ebook) | LCC PE1450 .W38 2019 (print) | DDC 428.2/3—dc23
LC record available at https://lccn.loc.gov/2018045968

ISBN 978-0-06-285305-9

19 20 21 22 23 LSC 10 9 8 7 6 5 4 3 2 1

For my parents,
who made sure I always had enough to read

Punctuation is a gentle and unobtrusive art that has long been one of the misfortunes of man. For about three hundred years it has been harassing him, and bewildering him with its quiet contrariness, and no amount of usage seems to make him grow in familiarity with the art.

"Power of Points: Punctuation That Upset Work of Solons," *Boston Daily Globe*, January 20, 1901

CONTENTS

LOVE, HATE, AND SEMICOLONS

"The semicolon has become so hateful to me," confessed Paul Robinson in a *New Republic* essay, "that I feel almost morally compromised when I use it." When Robinson, a humanities professor at Stanford, sees a dot balanced over a comma, he's filled with "exasperation." Robinson is perhaps the semicolon's most devoted foe, but he's hardly its only modern detractor. Novelists from George Orwell to Donald Barthelme have discoursed on its ugliness, or irrelevance, or both. Kurt Vonnegut was unequivocal in his last book, advising writers, "Do not use semicolons. They are transvestite hermaphrodites representing absolutely nothing. All they do is show you've been to college." And almost 800,000 people have shared a web comic that labels the semicolon "the most feared punctuation mark on earth." Yet when the Italian humanists invented the semicolon in the fifteenth century, they conceived of it as an aid to clarity, not (as Professor Robinson now characterizes it) a "pretentious" mark used chiefly to "gloss over an imprecise thought." In the late 1800s, the semicolon was downright *trendy*, its frequency of use far outstripping that of one of its relatives, the colon. How did the semicolon, once regarded with admiration, come to seem so offensive, so unwieldy, to so many people?

Asking this question might seem academic in all the worst ways: what practical value could there be in mulling punctuation, and in particular its history, when we have efficiently slim guidebooks like Strunk and White's *The Elements of Style* and thick reference volumes like *The Chicago Manual of Style* to set straight our misplaced colons and commas? We have *rules* for this sort of thing! But rule-based punctuation guides are a relatively recent invention. Prior to the 1800s, the majority of grammarians and scholars advocated personal taste and judgment as a guide to punctuating, or "pointing," a text. The Scottish Enlightenment philosopher George Campbell, writing the same year the Declaration of Independence was signed, argued that "language is purely a species of fashion. . . . It is not the business of grammar, as some critics seem preposterously to imagine, to give law to the fashions which regulate our speech."

But what Campbell and most of his contemporaries thought was a "preposterous" idea soon became a commonplace principle: as the 1700s drew to a close, new grammar books began to espouse systems of rules that were purportedly derived from logic. In these new books, grammarians didn't hesitate to impugn the grammar of writers traditionally considered great stylists: Milton and Shakespeare were chastised for "gross mistakes," and subjected to grammarians' emendations, so that these great authors' works were made to fall in line with rules established centuries after their deaths.

But a strange thing happened as the new genre of grammar rule books developed: instead of making people less confused about grammar, rule books seemed to cause *more* problems. No one knew *which* system of rules was the most correct one, and the more specific the grammarians made their guidelines for using punctuation marks like the semicolon, the more confusing those punctuation marks became. The more defined the function of the semicolon became, the more anxiety people experienced about when to use a semicolon in writing and how to interpret one while reading. Grammarians fought viciously over the supremacy of their individual sets of rules, scorching one another in the nineteenth-century equivalent of flame wars. Courts of law, too, were in a lather over how to deal with punctuation marks: a semicolon in an 1875 legal statute caused all of Boston to fly into a panic when courts opined that the semicolon meant that alcohol couldn't be served past 11:00 P.M. (Bostonians, ever resourceful, devised some pretty clever ways to get drunk well into the wee hours until the statute was finally revised six years after it went into force.)

The story of the semicolon told in these pages follows a chronological path, charting its transformation from a mark designed to create clarity to a mark destined to create confusion. The events described here epitomize the major steps in the life of the semicolon: they show how the semicolon transformed over time, and what was important about those transformations. That importance lies in the semicolon's ability to symbolize and trigger ideas and emotions that transcend the punctuation mark itself. The semicolon is a place where our anxieties and our aspirations about language, class, and education are concentrated, so that in this small mark big ideas are distilled down to a few winking drops of ink.

The semicolon's biography is also a story about grammar and language more generally—and this history will challenge the *myth* most of us like to tell ourselves about grammar. Grammar (in our mythical narrative) is part of the good old days: people used to know grammar *properly*, we think, the same way they used to walk three miles to school uphill in the snow, and everyone was polite and better-looking and thin and well-dressed. There are reasons these romantic visions of the past flourish in our collective consciousness: the stories of our grandparents; old black-and-white portraits that freeze the past in Sunday best; and most powerfully of all, a vague shared sense that the world is growing less innocent and less coherent, and that the past must therefore be better the farther back uphill into it we are able to climb. Things were harder in some ways back then, we acknowledge; but weren't they also better and purer, too?

"It's tough being a stickler for grammar these days," sighs Lynne Truss in *Eats, Shoots and Leaves*, as if before "these days" there was a time when everyone was committed to proper grammar and everyone agreed on what proper grammar constituted. Self-styled grammar "sticklers," "snobs," "nazis," and "bitches" want so much to get back to that point in the past where the majority of people respected language and understood its nuances, and society at large shared a common understanding of grammar rules. But that place is a mirage. There was no time when everyone spoke flawless English and people punctuated "properly." It's important to come to grips with this historical fact, because it influences how we act in the present: after we nail down some basic punctuation history here through the story of the semicolon, I'll show that hanging on to the old story about grammar—the mythical story—limits our relationship with language. It keeps us from seeing, describing, and creating beauty in language that rules can't comprehend.

I wouldn't deny that there's joy in knowing a set of

grammar rules; there is always joy in mastery of some branch of knowledge. But there is much *more* joy in becoming a reader who can understand and explain how it is that a punctuation mark can create meaning in language that goes beyond just delineating the logical structure of a sentence. Great punctuation can create music, paint a picture, or conjure emotions. This book will show you how the semicolon is essential to the effectiveness and aesthetic appeal of passages from Herman Melville, Raymond Chandler, Henry James, Irvine Welsh, Rebecca Solnit, and other masters of English fiction and nonfiction. Looking at these authors, we will see beautiful uses of the semicolon that cannot be adequately encapsulated in grammarians' rules, nor explained simply as a "breaking" of those rules.

Still, inadequate and artificial as grammar rules are, I understand what it's like to love them. In fact, I'm a reformed grammar fetishist myself, the sort of person who used to feel that her love for English was best expressed by means of irritation at the sight of a misplaced apostrophe, or outright heart palpitations over a comma splice. My own dive into the history of the semicolon was precipitated by a fight over one that my PhD adviser, Bob,[*] had circled in one of my papers, alleging that it violated the precepts of *The Chicago Manual of Style* (at the time, Bob was chair of the board of the press that publishes the *Manual*). I insisted that the semicolon in question was a perfectly legitimate interpretation of one of the umpteen semicolon rules the *Manual* laid out, and round and round Bob and I went for weeks, grandstanding about the meaning of the *Manual*'s rules. Finally, during one of these heated debates, it occurred to me to wonder: *Where do these rules I cherish so much, and believe I know so well, come from?*

Answering that question took me on a ten-year journey through piles of dusty grammar books that had lain untouched on library shelves for decades, and more often centuries. Some, having been forgotten for so long, collapsed in my hands; others left my palms tinted a guilty red with rot from their decaying leather bindings. But the words inside those old grammar

---

[*] Robert J. Richards at the University of Chicago. As of March 28, 2018, Bob's entry on Wikipedia contains semicolon usage that I'm quite certain would rankle him: "Richards earned two PhDs; one in the History of Science from the University of Chicago and another in Philosophy from St. Louis University." Bob, I swear it wasn't me!

books had lost none of their liveliness and passion, and I soon became absorbed in the drama of grammarians' attempts to create a market for their rules in the face of an initially skeptical public. The story that I began to piece together from their pages called on all my skills as an academic. It demanded my expertise in the history of science: grammar rules, it turns out, began as an attempt to "scientize" language, because science was what parents wanted their children taught in public schools. Equally, the story of the semicolon called on my training in philosophy, as I began to wonder what ethical imperatives knowing the true history of grammar rules might impose. And finally, crucial to making sense of the story of the semicolon were my years of experience teaching writing at institutions like Yale, the University of Chicago, and Bard College.

By the time I had finished writing the story contained in these pages, I had changed everything about how I looked at grammar. I still love language, but I love it in a richer way. Not only did I become a better and more sensitive reader and a more capable teacher, I also became a better person. Perhaps that sounds like a fancifully hyperbolic claim—can changing our relationship with grammar really make us better human beings? By the end of this book, I hope to persuade you that reconsidering grammar rules will do exactly that, by refocusing us on the deepest, most primary value and purpose of language: true communication and openness to others.

But before I can try to persuade you of this, we have to look the past square in the face. Ever since grammar rules were invented, they have caused at least as much confusion and distress as they have ameliorated; and people living one hundred years ago had passions about semicolons that varied from decade to decade and person to person. In this regard, they aren't so different from us after all: when you looked at the semicolons on the front of this book, you probably felt something. Was it hate, like Paul Robinson? Anger? Love? Curiosity? Confusion? The diminutive semicolon can inspire great passion. As you'll see in the chapters that follow, it always has.

I

DEEP HISTORY

The Birth of the Semicolon

The semicolon was born in Venice in 1494. It was meant to signify a pause of a length somewhere between that of the comma and that of the colon, and this heritage was reflected in its form, which combines half of each of those marks. It was born into a time period of writerly experimentation and invention, a time when there were no punctuation rules, and readers created and discarded novel punctuation marks regularly. Texts (both handwritten and printed) record the testing-out and tinkering-with of punctuation by the fifteenth-century literati known as the Italian humanists. The humanists put a premium on eloquence and excellence in writing, and they called for the study and retranscription of Greek and Roman classical texts as a way to effect a "cultural rebirth" after the gloomy Middle Ages. In the service of these two goals, humanists published new writing and revised, repunctuated, and reprinted classical texts.

One of these humanists, Aldus Manutius, was the matchmaker who paired up comma and colon to create the semicolon. Manutius was a printer and publisher, and the first literary Latin text he issued was *De Aetna*, by his contemporary Pietro Bembo. *De Aetna* was an essay, written in dialogue form, about climbing volcanic Mount Etna in Italy. On its pages lay a new hybrid mark, specially cut for this text by Bolognese type designer Francesco Griffo: the semicolon (and Griffo dreamed up a nice plump version) is sprinkled here and there throughout the text, conspiring with colons, commas, and parentheses to aid readers.

In this snippet, you can see four of these brand-new semicolons. You might think you see eight, but beware! That semicolonish mark at the end of the fourth line from the bottom isn't a semicolon, it's an abbreviation for *que*, Latin for "and." In this case, it's

helping to shorten *neque*, or "also not." It appears elsewhere in in the excerpt, always filling in the -ue part
of a *que*. If you look closely, you'll see that the dot-and-
curve combination is raised higher up than a semicolon; it's positioned on the same level as the words in

> politani etiam tractus extimantur. Ni-
> uibus per hyemem ferè totus mons ca-
> net:cacumen neq; per aeſtatem uiduatur.
> B. P. Quid,quod hyemare tantum
> eas meminit Strabo? B. F. At experien
> tia ita te docet,uſq; ipſe auctor (quod qui
> dem uenia illius dixerim) non deterior.
> Quare illud mi páter etiá,atq; etiam uide;
> ne quid te moueat,ſi aliqua ex parte huius
> noſtri de Aetna ſermonis cum uetuſtis ſcri
> ptoribus diſſentimus:nihil enim impedit
> fuiſſe tum ea omnia,quae ipſi olim tradi
> dere,quorum permáſerint plurima in no
> ſtram diem;quaedam ſe immutauerít;alí
> qua etiam ſurrexerint noua:nam(ut caete
> ra ómittam); quod cineroſa partim eſſe
> ſumma cacumina dictauere;eius rei nunc
> ueſtigium nullú apparet:cinis enim,qui
> queat conſpici,toto móte nullus eſt:neq;
> id tamen omnibus annis fuit: nam mul
> torum teſtimonio accepimus,qui ui-
> dere, annos ab hinc quadraginta tan-

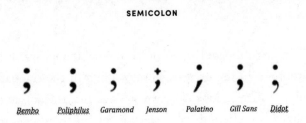

Bembo   Poliphilus   Garamond   Jenson   Palatino   Gill Sans   Didot

the text because it's shorthand for a word instead of a signal to pause.

Nearly as soon as the ink was dry on those first semicolons, they began to proliferate, and newly cut font families began to include them as a matter of course. The Bembo typeface's tall semicolon was the original that appeared in *De Aetna*, with its comma-half tensely coiled, tail thorn-sharp beneath the perfect orb thrown high above it. The semicolon in Poliphilus, relaxed and fuzzy, looks casual in comparison, like a Keith Haring character taking a break from buzzing. Garamond's semicolon is watchful, aggressive, and elegant, its lower half a cobra's head arced back to strike. Jenson's is a simple shooting star. We moderns have accumulated a host of characterful semicolons to choose from: Palatino's is a thin flapper in a big hat slouched against the wall at a party. Gill Sans MT's semicolon has perfect posture, while Didot's puffs its chest out pridefully. (For the postmodernist writer Donald Barthelme, none of these punch-cut* disguises could ever conceal the semicolon's innate hideousness: to him it was "ugly, ugly as a tick on a dog's belly.")

The semicolon had successfully colonized the letter cases of the best presses in Europe, but other newborn punctuation marks were not so lucky. The humanists tried out a lot of new punctuation ideas, but most of those marks had short life spans. Some of the printed texts that appeared in the centuries surrounding the semicolon's birth look as though they are written partially in secret code: they are filled with mysterious dots, dashes, swoops, and curlicues. There were marks for the minutest distinctions and the most specific occasions. For instance, there was once a *punctus percontativus*, or rhetorical question mark, which was a mirror-image version of the question mark. Why did the semicolon survive and thrive when other marks did not? Probably because it was *useful*. Readers, writers,

---

* Back in the humanists' day, the letters for a font were carved into steel bars. These were called "punches." The technique was punch cutting, and its practitioner a punch cutter.

and printers found that the semicolon was worth the trouble to insert. The rhetorical question mark, on the other hand, faltered and then fizzled out completely. This isn't too surprising: does anyone really need a special punctuation mark to know when a question is rhetorical?

In humanist times, just as in our own, hand-wringing sages forecast a literary apocalypse precipitated by too-casual attitudes to punctuation. "It is not concealed from you how great a shortage there is of intelligent scribes in these times," wrote one French humanist to another,

> and above all in transcribing those things which observe style to any degree; in which unless points and marks of *distinctions*, by which the style flows through the *cola*, *commata*, and *periodi*, are separated with more attentive diligence, that which is written is confused and barbarous. . . . Which carelessness, in my opinion, has occurred chiefly since we have for a long time lacked eloquence, in which these things are necessary: the ancient manner of handwriting, therefore, in which the scribes of books (*antiquarii*) were

gradually writing a perfect and correctly formed script with precise punctuation (*certa distinctione*) of *clausulae* and with notes of accentuation, has perished together with the art of expression (*dictatu*).

The entire art of expression—dead, because careless writers just couldn't hack it when it came to punctuation. Well, I think we moderns might maintain that the art of expression gave us a few rather decent literary works even after the date of this fifteenth-century letter. But the lament of the French humanists is familiar, isn't it? People can't punctuate correctly, eloquence is slowly dying out. *Plus ça change* . . .

Still, a few cranky complainants notwithstanding, most humanists believed that each writer should work out his punctuation for himself,* rather than employing a predetermined set of rules. A writer or an annotating reader was to exercise his own taste and judgment. This idea of punctuation as a matter of individual taste and style outlived the humanists: it stretched beyond

---

* In those days, it was usually a "him," although there were of course exceptions.

the Latin texts that Manutius printed, crossing borders and oceans, and it survived as a way of thinking about the practice of punctuation well into the eighteenth century. When the topic of punctuation usage came up, a reader was likely to be advised that he should consider the punctuation marks analogous to rests in music, and deploy them according to the musical effect he wanted to achieve. How on earth did this idea of the writer as musician, which held on for hundreds of years, transform into our comparatively new expectation that writers must submit to rigid rules?

II

THE SCIENCE OF SEMICOLONS

American Grammar Wars

Goold Brown, schoolteacher and grammar obsessive, had a lofty ambition: he wanted to produce "something like a complete grammar of the English language." Twenty-seven years after first resolving to undertake this task, he finally published *The Grammar of English Grammars*, which contained 1,192 pages filled with tiny print surveying *a selection** of 548 English grammar

---

* I'm surprised he could bring himself to use a selection. Brown was a thorough guy, the type of person who dated his copy of

books that had been published in the eighteenth and nineteenth centuries, up until the 1851 printing of his own book.*

Where were all of these grammar books that Goold Brown surveyed coming from, and what had made them explode in number so suddenly, after several quiet centuries of minimal punctuation guidance for writers? A jaunt through some of the most popular grammar books of the nineteenth century will reveal that their authors were shrewd entrepreneurs taking advantage of a newly developed and highly lucrative market for education in English writing. They were also masters of the biting insult, as they jockeyed for position (and market share) with one another. And— perhaps most surprisingly—they were aspiring *scientists*. We have to understand the great shift these authors created in the way people thought about English grammar in order to understand the semicolon's transfor-

---

Churchill's *English Grammar* "A.D. 1824," lest anyone mistakenly think he might have bought it in 1824 B.C.

* My copy of Goold's compendium is a menacing leather-bound brick measuring $9\,{}^{3}/_{4}$ inches by $6\,{}^{1}/_{2}$ inches by 3 inches and tipping the scales at 4 pounds, 15 ounces. It's caused my checked baggage to violate airline weight allowances on three occasions.

mation: although these first professional grammarians sought clarity through rules, they ended up creating confusion, and the semicolon was collateral damage.

The first English grammar book to achieve lasting influence and popularity by creating laws for language was Robert Lowth's 1758 *A Short Introduction to English Grammar.* Lowth boldly announced that it was his aim to "lay down rules" for grammar. These rules, he felt, were usually best presented by showing violations of them along with judicious corrections. Accordingly, he assembled examples from some of the very worst syntactical offenders available in English at the time, true

---

(1) Some Writers have ufed *Ye* as the Objective Cafe Plural of the Pronoun of the Second Perfon; very improperly, and ungrammatically.

" The more fhame for *ye :* holy men I thought *ye.*"
         Shakfpeare, Hen. VIII.

" But tyrants dread *ye,* left your juft degree
'Transfer the pow'r, and fet the people free."
            Prior.

" His wrath, which one day will deftroy *ye* both. "
         Milton, P. L. ii. 734.

Milton ufes the fame manner of expreffion in a few other places of his Paradife Loft, and more frequently in his

---

Shakespeare and Milton, both very improper!

> " Oft have I feen a timely-parted ghoſt,
> Of aſhy femblance, meagre, pale, and bloodleſs,
> Being all defcended to the lab'ring heart,
> *Who*, in the conflict that *it* holds with death,
> Attracts the fame for aidance 'gainſt the enemy."
>
> Shakefpear, 2 Hen. VI.
>
> It ought to be,
> " *Which*, in the conflict that *it* holds "——
> Or, perhaps more poetically,
> " *Who*, in the conflict that *he* holds with death."

Lowth giving Shakespeare a little lesson in grammar and poetry writing.*

grammatical failures including Shakespeare, Donne, Pope, Swift, and Milton.

Even though Lowth didn't hesitate to perpetrate brow-raising "corrections" on writers who seem, well, pretty competent, he did still carry with him the legacy of the previous centuries' emphasis on personal

---

* You will notice an odd typographical quirk in Lowth's text: the "Medial S," which looks to the modern eye like an "f" but is to be read as an "s." The Medial S can lead to some unintentionally seedy reading in books that are reprinted in facsimile edition, like Antoine Lavoisier's *Elements of Chemistry*, which contains a long section in which the author describes sucking air through a tube for an experiment.

taste and style, and he reserved a place for individual discretion, particularly when it came to punctuation. For punctuation, he acknowledged, "few precise rules can be given, which will hold without exception in all cases; but much must be left to the judgment and taste of the writer." As we've seen before, the marks of punctuation were analogous to the rests in a piece of music, and were to be applied as individual circumstances and preferences dictated. The comma thus was a pause shorter than the semicolon, and the semicolon was a pause shorter than the colon.

Lowth's book reigned supreme for a couple of decades, until another grammarian, Lindley Murray, came along and decided he could probably sell a few books himself if he tweaked Lowth's work a bit by increasing its structural precision and its rigidity. In order to rebuild the book in this way, he divided it into sections and numbered its rules. Murray retitled this new version *English Grammar.* To say that *English Grammar* was a blockbuster success is an understatement. The book went into twenty-four editions, reprinted by sixteen different American publishers between 1797 and 1870, and it sold so many copies that Murray was "the best-selling producer of books *in the world*" between 1800 and 1840.

Just as Murray found success renovating Lowth's foundations, so Murray's grammar had some additions nailed on by another upstart grammarian, Samuel Kirkham. Kirkham's 1823 grammar gradually displaced its archetype. Where Murray's grammar had gone into a dizzying twenty-four editions, Kirkham's went into at least *one hundred and ten*. Kirkham won over readers by presenting a new system of parsing verbs, and by extending his predecessors' criticisms of "false syntax" in historical English. Even as Kirkham's book represented a further step towards *more* rules and *more* systematization, the very first edition of his grammar omitted punctuation entirely, on the grounds that it was part of prosody rather than grammar: in other words, punctuation was all about establishing rhythm, intonation, and stresses. This stance got Kirkham some critical reviews, however; as a consequence, subsequent editions covered punctuation—but only briefly, and only by nebulously describing punctuation marks as pauses of varying lengths. Thus, for the king of nineteenth-century grammar-book sales, punctuation remained a tool that writers could wield with a good bit of flexibility and discretion.

With sales of his book so high, Kirkham was in the spotlight. Not only did that open him up to attack, but it even allowed him to cultivate a proper *nemesis*. That nemesis was Goold Brown, the grammar surveyor in whose gargantuan book Kirkham was but one of hundreds of other people plying the same trade. But out of all those grammarians, Kirkham was the one who most got under Brown's skin. As Brown saw it, Kirkham had played fast and loose with grammar, and cared more about his bottom line than about scientific scruples: he wanted to "veer his course according to the *trade-wind*," Brown sniped. In Brown's eyes, when Kirkham revised his grammar book to include punctuation, the additions represented not honest scholarly progression but mercenary modifications: "his whole design" was a "paltry scheme of present income." And—Brown added—Kirkham's character was such that he was "filled with glad wonder at his own popularity." Labeling Kirkham a quack and a plagiarist, Brown tore into his grammar book on page after page, pointing out its logical contradictions and omissions. Interspersed with these *ad librum* jabs are some choice *ad hominem* sucker punches. In one particularly efficient passage, Brown calls out Kirkham's reasoning while also claiming that he didn't write his own book *and* insinuating that he was too cheap to pay his ghostwriter adequately:

> As a grammarian, Kirkham claims to be second only to Lindley Murray; and says, "Since the days of Lowth, no other work on grammar, Murray's only excepted, has been so favorably received by the *publick* as his own. As a proof of this, he would mention, that within the last six years it has passed through *fifty* editions."—*Preface to Elocution*, p. 12. And, at the same time, and in the same preface, he complains, that, "Of all the labors done under the sun, the labors *of the pen* meet with the poorest reward."—*Ibid.*, p. 5. This too clearly favours the report, that his books were not written by himself, but by others whom he hired. Possibly, the anonymous helper may here have penned, not his employer's feeling, but a line of his own experience. But I choose to ascribe the passage to the professed author, and to hold him answerable for the inconsistency.

Kirkham answered Brown's complaints about his boasting with . . . more boasting, this time underlined with populist rhetoric.

> What! A book have no merit, and yet be called for at the rate of *sixty thousand copies a year*! What a slander is this upon the public taste! What an insult to the understanding and discrimination of the good people of these United States! According to this reasoning, all the inhabitants of our land must be fools, except one man, and that man is GOOLD BROWN!

Brown bit back, pointing out that Lord Byron got paid a lot more for *Childe Harold* than Milton did for *Paradise Lost;* but would anyone say *Byron* was the greater literary genius?

Brown and Kirkham may have pitted themselves against one another,* but they (along with their

---

* When Brown wasn't tearing up the work of other grammarians, he made his own constructive suggestions for reform. One of my favorites of his ideas was to rename the exclamation

contemporaries) agreed on one thing: grammar was to be viewed not as a mere matter of personal taste or style, but now as a coherent system of knowledge. Accordingly, they termed grammar a "science." But in the middle of the nineteenth century, a new wave of grammarians began to argue that grammar wasn't just a science in this broad sense of schematic knowledge, but a science in the narrower sense in which we use the word nowadays. To these new grammarians, their field was analogous to the natural sciences.

In staking this claim, the new grammarian-scientists were almost certainly reacting to protests from parents of schoolchildren and school officials, who claimed that the study of grammar was boring and ineffectual; pupils' time was better spent studying the natural sciences, which were exciting and taught *real* skills. Complaints about the mind-numbing uselessness of grammar surfaced as early as 1827, came to a boil by 1850, and simmered through the rest of the nineteenth century. If grammarians wanted to stay relevant

---

point the "eroteme," since it is a mark of passion. (From the Greek ἔρως [eros], meaning "love" or "desire.")

and sell those lucrative grammar books to schools and their pupils, they needed to answer to carping parents and officials. The grammarians' solution was rather ingenious: grammar, they proposed, was a method of teaching students the art of scientific observation without requiring expensive or complex scientific apparatus. In service of this goal of teaching scientific skills, grammarians resolved to employ careful observation of English as a way to use the methods of science to refine grammar; and they imported into their grammars some of the conventions of science textbooks, like diagrams.

Rebel grammarian Isaiah J. Morris emphasized the first approach—careful observation of English—in his 1858 *Morris's grammar. A philosophical and practical grammar of the English language, dialogically and progressively arranged; in which every word is parsed according to its use.** Morris came out swinging from the start, distancing himself from reigning champions

---

* Believe it or not, this is a relatively pithy title for a nineteenth-century book; some of them really took the term *title page* to be an imperative to fill the whole sheet.

of grammar like the bestselling Samuel Kirkham. Kirkham and his ilk had relied on Greek and Latin grammar to come up with rules for English, and as a result, Morris fumed, they had littered the true "laws of language" with "errors" and "absurdities," which Morris was now left to "expose and explode." Correcting these mistakes was a moral obligation: "Shall we roll sin under our tongues as a sweet morsel?" Morris demanded. "It must be sin to teach what we know to be error." In order to cleanse English grammars of these corruptions, Morris devoted the preface of his grammar to eviscerating the stale precepts of his predecessors. He knew that shredding such venerable grammarians would shock his readers: "If the truth be disagreeable," he shrugged, "I choose to be offensive."[*]

Morris offered a way to get beyond the deference to Latin and Greek that he believed had made earlier grammarians so error-prone: he advocated observing English carefully, and then making rules based on those observations, rather than trying to squeeze

---

[*] Morris is probably my favorite grammarian. What can I say? I like a sharp-spoken rebel.

PREFACE

IT is often said that English Grammar is a lifetime study, **and** it is a fact not to be disguised, that students usually prosecute this branch of science for years, to little practical purpose, as grammar pupils rarely speak or write more correctly than others untaught. Now, grammar is unworthy of a lifetime study ; life is too important, and labor and money are too precious to be thus invested, or, rather, wasted. "Time is money."—DR. FRANKLIN.

Is it not a little curious, that English Grammar should be a lifetime study? If so, who has yet mastered it? Who is competent to teach it? One would make rather an unprofitable effort, trying to teach what he did not understand himself. Would it not be more than unkind to require children to recite, and expect them to comprehend, what neither teachers nor authors understand, or can explain?

Isaiah J. Morris, "offensive" from the very first page

English grammar into frameworks designed for dead languages.* Grammar rules would then arise directly

---

* Morris, as a "new grammarian" committed to observation of English, left Pope and Milton alone, unlike his predecessors. Instead of correcting the classics, the new generation of grammarians decided to amend each other's work instead, sometimes to absurd and comical effect. Alfred Ayres, a grammarian and elocutionist who edited an 1893 edition of *The English Grammar of William Cobbett*, praised the book as "probably the most readable grammar ever written." Nonetheless, Ayres demurred, Cobbett's grammar had become a little bit dated in the fifty years that had passed since it was first printed. Ayres, as editor,

from scrutinizing English in action—and conveniently enough, the study of grammar would thus acquire for itself some of the virtues of the natural sciences that were being championed in the press, where commentators regularly argued that students were inherently inclined towards the observation and study of natural phenomena.

Grammarians had a second strategy to advance against critics who complained about the inferiority of grammar when compared to the natural sciences: the sentence diagram. Any good science textbook had diagrams, and if grammar was to be a science, it surely needed a system of schematic illustrations as well. And so in 1847, a grammarian named Stephen Clark introduced

---

felt it was his duty to repair Cobbett's mistakes by inserting bracketed corrections throughout the book. Thus Ayres turned this example sentence from Cobbett's original:

"And that it was this which made that false which would otherwise have been, and which was intended to be, true!"

into

"And that it was this which [that] made that false which [that] would otherwise have been, and which [that] was intended to be, true!"

So much for Cobbett's vaunted "readability."

a system of diagrams designed to relate to the "Science of Language" as maps did to geography, and figures to geometry and arithmetic. (It might sound odd to the modern reader to think of geography and geometry as natural sciences like physics and chemistry, but plenty of people back in Clark's days thought of them that way, and even people who didn't categorize those areas of study as "sciences" believed the two disciplines were essential for the study of both the natural sciences and other respected fields like philosophy. And unlike grammar, the mathematical sciences were considered "perfect" and "useful.")

Clark's diagrams often made use of Bible verses: might as well pack in a few fearsome reminders about

"*The Lord uplifts his awful hand
And chains you to the shore.*"
(15.)

Compound sentence—transitive.

ANALYSIS.

Principal parts. {
Lord—Subject of "uplifts" and "chains."
Uplifts
[And] } Predicates of "Lord."
Chains
Hand—Object of "uplifts."
You—Object of "chains."
}

Adjuncts. {
The—Adjunct of "Lord."
His
Awful } Adjuncts of "hand."
To the shore—Adjunct of "chains."
}

the powers of the Almighty for those schoolchildren misbehaving in the back of the class, after all.

The diagrams were a popular addition to grammar books, and held on for a long time. Although they've fallen out of pedagogical fashion these days, some readers may remember grammar classes from their childhoods that relied heavily on diagramming sentences on the chalkboard. I certainly do, although I don't recall ever having to produce anything quite so comically elaborate as this doozy:

EXAMPLES OF COMPLEX SENTENCES.

☞ **Rem.**—Let the pupil write the Diagram for each sentence on the black-board and insert the words in the proper places.

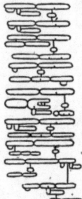

Blessed are the poor in spirit,

for theirs is the kingdom of heaven.

Blessed are they that mourn,

for they shall be comforted.
Blessed are the meek,
for they shall inherit the earth.

Blessed are they which do hunger and thirst
after righteousness, for they shall be filled.
Blessed are the pure in heart,
for they shall see God.
Blessed is the man that endureth temptation,
for, when he is tried,

he shall receive the crown of life,
which the Lord hath promised
to them that love him.

Clark, who invented the sentence-diagramming technique to visualize language, did his best to make the rest of his grammar follow the definitive-sounding, principle- and fact-heavy aesthetic of the natural sciences in other ways, too. Clark's rules were set up in an outline form, which Clark borrowed from his contemporary Peter Bullions. Bullions had used outlines to show his readers "leading principles, definitions, and rules." Those rules were to be displayed "in larger type" to emphasize their importance; and exceptions to the rules were printed in type that got smaller and smaller the further away from an ironclad principle they crept.

In Bullions's nesting-doll fonts a fundamental tension is writ large: the conflicting demands of *rules* and *taste*. Bullions wrote that the purpose of punctuation was "to convey to the reader an exact sense, and assist him in the proper delivery." He warned, however, in a font two points smaller, that "the duration of the pauses must be left to the taste of the reader or speaker." Nevertheless, he then provided twenty-five rules and exceptions for the comma alone. These rules were then followed by yet another disclaimer in an even tinier font than the first: "The foregoing rules will, it is hoped, be found comprehensive; yet there may be

152   ENGLISH GRAMMAR.   § 88

466. The principal stops are the following:

The Comma (,) the semicolon (;) the colon (:) the period, or full stop (.) the note of interrogation (!) the note of exclamation (!)

467. The comma represents the shortest pause; the semicolon, a pause double that of the comma; the colon, double that of the semicolon; and the period, double that of the colon.

468. The duration of the pauses must be left to the taste of the reader or speaker.

493. When, however, these phrases are not considered important, and particularly in short sentences, the comma is not inserted; as, "There is *surely* a pleasure in acting kindly." "Idleness *certainly* is the mother of all vices." "He was *at last* convinced of his error."

494.₊*₊The foregoing rules will, it is hoped, be found comprehensive; yet there may be some cases in which the student must rely on his own judgment.

Bullions and the tension between rules and taste

some cases in which the student must rely on his own judgment." Bullions seems to be equivocating, vacillating between committing to rules on the one hand, and capitulating to taste on the other.

Bullions's dilemma was *every* nineteenth-century grammarian's debacle: how could it be possible to give useful rules for punctuation, while at the same time acknowledging that those rules couldn't describe every valid approach to punctuating a text? Whether a grammarian tried to police English with the laws of ancient Latin and Greek, or instead to derive his principles from examination of contemporary English in action, he could not escape the tension between the rigidity of rules and the flexibility of usage. Even if English writers' actual practices were taken into account and described in the rules, once laid down, the rules couldn't shift, while usage inevitably did. The grammarian was necessarily torn between trying (and inevitably failing) to anticipate every kind of usage, as Peter Bullions did with his twenty-five comma rules; or giving rules so general they were scarcely rules at all, the strategy Robert Lowth opted for with his specification that punctuation marks were successively longer pauses.*

---

* People like Robert Lowth are typically termed "prescriptivists," and grammarians like Isaiah Morris "descriptivists." Prescriptivists give rules about how language *ought* to be, while descriptivists want to observe and describe language. These

Mega-meta-grammarian Goold Brown, in his exhaustive *Grammar of English Grammars*, attempted to honey this problem with a bit of aspirational rhetoric.

> Some may begin to think that in treating of grammar we are dealing with something too various and changeable for the understanding to grasp; a dodging Proteus of the imagination, who is ever ready to assume some new shape, and elude the vigilance of the inquirer. But let the reader or student do his part; and, if he please, follow us with attention. We will endeavor, with

---

categories are unfairly extreme in the case of nineteenth-century grammarians. They give the impression that supposed prescriptivists (like Lowth and his adherents) laid down laws without recognizing that a writer's *taste* was still important, and they give the impression that supposed descriptivists (Morris and his ilk) just described language in action without trying to give any laws. The truth is much more complicated. All of these grammarians, negotiating the competing demands of rules and personal taste, were much more nuanced than dumping them into prescriptivist or descriptivist camps would indicate. In fact, one of the things that's most fascinating about reading grammars from Lowth's and Morris's times is how plain it is on the face of the texts that the grammarians were struggling with this fundamental problem of grammar.

welded links, to bind this Proteus, in such a manner that he shall neither escape from our hold, nor fail to give to the consulter an intelligible and satisfactory response. Be not discouraged, generous youth.

Brown's labors may have been Herculean in scope, but they were still insufficient to solidify the fluid laws of grammar. Whenever grammarians tried to pin down punctuation marks with rules, they inevitably slipped their restraints, no matter whether they were shackled with a few broad rules or a hundred narrow ones. This Proteus didn't stop shifting shapes, it was just that now he had a heavy chain awkwardly dangling from his heels as he did so. The thorny relationship between rules and usage came to play a major role in the fate of our hero, the semicolon.

III.

SEXY SEMICOLONS

In early spring of 1857, a writer for the *Chicago Daily Tribune* took a stroll through the streets of Chicago, making a note of facial hair trends for an article in the paper. Particularly popular was a mustache combined with a small goatee: "Forty-three wore the moustache with a fancy tuft upon the chin, but with smooth cheeks; looking as if a semicolon was the best representation of their idea of facial adornment."

The comparison was apt: semicolons were trendy in any form, follicular or literary.

For those of you accustomed to thinking about

punctuation as subject to rules, it probably sounds odd to suggest that punctuation usage could be subject to shifts in fashion. One of the virtues of rules would be to insulate us from whims and fancies. But even the originators of rule-based punctuation guides, the grammarians we encountered in the previous chapter, copped to punctuation's trendiness. As we saw, they were conflicted about how best to negotiate the tension between rules and actual usage. As a result of their examination of usage, grammarians became keen observers of the punctuation whims of writers. The semicolon was on the rise in the 1800s, and its popularity might have been linked to the *un*fashionableness of two other marks, the parenthesis and the colon. By the early 1800s, parentheses were already *so* last century, inspiring T. O. Churchill's 1823 grammar to coolly pronounce that "the parenthesis is now generally exploded as a deformity." It got worse: three years later, the parenthesis had gone from Quasimodo to quasi ghost, with Rufus Nutting's *Practical Grammar* and Bradford Frazee's *Improved Grammar* both deeming it "nearly obsolete." The curved marks that humanist thinker Desiderius Erasmus had romantically called "little moons" (lunulae) had crashed down to earth. By the mid-1800s, writers were also snubbing the colon: Oliver Felton's 1843 grammar fobbed it off with "The COLON is now so seldom used by good writers, that rules for its use are unnecessary." Seven years later, *The Common School Journal* gravely advised that when it came to colons, "we should not let children use them," and "should advise advanced scholars seldom to use them."

This bad news for the colon was excellent news for the semicolon, however. It was the semicolon that writers substituted for its unstylish progenitor, and the semicolon soon surged through sentences at such a pace that it gobbled up not just most of the colons but a large share of commas as well. The semicolon had gotten so fashionable by the 1840s that Goold Brown leveraged its appeal to implore writers to reconsider the now-neglected colon. "But who cannot perceive," begged Brown, "that without the colon, the semicolon becomes an absurdity? It can no longer be a semicolon, unless the half can remain when the whole is taken away!" Brown pointed out that there was really nothing wrong with the colon anyway; after all, he argued, colons, too, were "once very fashionable." (Brown himself was not, however, immune to the seductions of

the semicolon: the first sentence of his massive grammar compendium contained seven of them, and nary a
colon.)

Although Brown appealed to fashion in his plea for
the colon, his argument offered a glimpse into the future of punctuation—the future we've inherited—in
which logic reigns supreme in guides to punctuating.
By the time that grammatical great H. W. Fowler
published *A Dictionary of Modern English Usage*, in 1926,
Brown's halves and wholes and absurdities had been
pressed by Fowler into sterile language reminiscent of
a *reductio* proof in mathematics, a curtly logical formu-
lation in which neither fashion nor taste nor passion
nor prosody had any part:

> The use of the semicolon to separate parallel
> expressions that would normally be separated by
> commas is not in itself illegitimate; but it must
> not be done when the expressions so separated
> form a group that is to be separated by nothing
> more than a comma, or not separated at all, from
> another part of the sentence; to do it is to make
> the less include the greater, which is absurd.

The semicolon had been transformed: before the 1800s, it had been a pause. By the early 1800s, grammarians began to describe these pauses as means to delineate clauses properly, such that punctuation served syntax, with its prosodic and musical features secondary. By the mid-1800s, guided by a new generation of grammarians, grammar was tiptoeing towards a natural science model, deriving its rules from observation of English and teaching those rules to students through exercises in which they would be guided to make the same observations and draw general conclusions from them in the form of rules.

This process of moving from particular examples to general principles is known as "induction." Faced with the shift towards an inductive method modeled on science, midcentury grammarians waffled on the proper place of punctuation in their guidebooks. Was punctuation part of orthography, the study of how a language should be written? Was it part of prosody, how language should sound? Or did punctuation fall under the heading of syntax, the study of how language should be structured? The problem sparked vigorous debate. If punctuation were to be part of prosody, how could it be taught with the properly scientific inductive method? A student could hardly be expected to inductively derive rules from the rich, subtle, and infinitely varied rhythms that punctuation created in texts!

Uncertain of punctuation's proper classification, some grammarians simply left it out of their books entirely, sidestepping the problem of making rules that would be appropriate for an observation-based, natural science of language. Where punctuation *was* included in mid-1800s manuals, however, writers were given ample opportunity for semicolon use. In George Payn Quackenbos's 1862 *An English Grammar*, four possibilities for semicolon usage were given, and students were instructed to use a semicolon (not a colon, as we moderns would) to introduce a list of items.

Most grammarians considered it perfectly acceptable to link together an independent and a dependent clause, so that the parts of the sentence sitting on either side of the semicolon didn't have to be able to stand on their own grammatically, each with a complete subject and verb. If the author thought it sounded right, no need to meddle. As grammarians' push towards logic, natural science, and induction continued, however, punctuation became decoupled from prosody and

THE SEMICOLON.

696. *Rule I.*—A semicolon must be placed between the members of compound sentences, unless the connection is exceedingly close; as "The wheel of fortune is ever turning; who can say, 'I shall be uppermost to-morrow'?"

If the members are very short, and the connection is close, the comma may be used in stead of the semicolon; as, "Man proposes, but God disposes."

697. *Rule II.*—A semicolon must be placed between the great divisions of sentences, when minor divisions occur that are separated by commas; as, "Plato called beauty a privilege of nature; Theocritus, a delightful prejudice."

698. *Rule III.*—A semicolon must be placed before an enumeration of particulars, when the names of the objects merely are given, without any formal introductory words; as, "There are three cases; the nominative, the possessive, and the objective."

699. *Rule IV.*—A semicolon must be placed before *as*, when it introduces an example; as at the close of the last paragraph.

Quackenbos's rules for the semicolon

personal preference. By the 1880s, grammarians distinguished between rhetorical pauses, which were akin to pauses in speaking and were not to be marked by punctuation; and grammatical pauses, which required punctuation in order to make the structural and logical attributes of a sentence clear.

There were a few holdouts who resisted the new model of grammar. W. C. Fowler, for instance, advocated applying punctuation marks to signal rhetorical pauses, and in his 1881 grammar, it was still permissible to use a semicolon between an independent and a dependent clause. But by his own admission, Fowler was the exception rather than the rule: by the time he published his book, grammarians were treating the semicolon like a controlled substance. They generally prescribed them only for use between independent clauses, or to separate items in a list that were long enough to be subdivided with commas. An 1888 report on punctuation by the California State Board of Education called attention to the fact that there was "but one use of the semicolon" in its lessons, its function restricted to separating independent clauses that contained commas. One hundred and thirty years had passed between Robert Lowth's grammar, which had envisioned punctuation marks as musical elements in prose, and this report, with its strict logic-based rules. In that time, the function of the semicolon had grown narrower and narrower until it had been whittled down to one or two applications.

This narrowing, as we've seen, happened in large part because grammar books were part of greater cultural and aesthetic trends in the Western world that privileged natural-scientific knowledge above other types of study; and in responding to those pressures, grammarians devised systems of punctuation that fit comfortably with the ideals and the formats employed in science textbooks. Where had a century of rules, of grammars labeled "true" and "real" and "improved," of grammars sidling up to natural science—where had all this gotten the generations of Americans who had grown up immersed in books devoted to these principles? Into trouble, that's where, according to commentators. "Where is the man that can tell why a comma is inserted instead of a semicolon; a semicolon, instead of a period; a colon, instead of a period?" asked an 1899 newspaper editorial. "And yet, the science of punctuation is almost as definite as the science of mathematics, and, with few exceptions, a reason can be given for every mark inserted." The rules were definitive, and yet their application varied wildly, and this divergence was apt to haunt a person all his or her life. As *The Boston Daily Globe* somberly intoned,

> From childhood's earliest hour, or from that early hour in which one graduates from pothooks and

hangers, and his wavering hand begins to form scraggly letters, those mysterious little hieroglyphics that must be placed somewhere in every sentence confront him, and confuse him, and all through his natural life get him in trouble. Then, perhaps, after death his heirs will call each other names and invoke the courts of law because he were indiscreet enough to use a comma where he should have put a semicolon.

The *Globe* had good reason to raise the specter of a punctuation-related legal battle; the new rule-based approach to punctuation had already begun to trouble the court system. Now it was not just the letter of the law but the punctuation separating those letters that judges and juries had to negotiate. Another commentator, for *The Indianapolis Journal*, concurred: citing four specific instances in which the semicolon had "made trouble in the laws" by creating ambiguity in statutes, the author ascribed this trouble to "inability to fix the function of the semicolon." Old grammar books had given the rules of punctuation in terms of pauses, and "if those who have been writing rules for punctuating compositions had stopped there, we would not have had all this trouble, but these teachers have been going on making new rules for years until no one can undertake to follow them, but each punctuates according to his pleasure, rather than his familiarity with the rules." Finding the rules unhelpful, the public had run screaming in the opposite direction, punctuating willy-nilly. Therefore, the commentator opined, either the court system should write a legal treatise to define punctuation marks once and for all, or it should resolve to ignore punctuation altogether in its rulings.

But unbeknownst to the commentator, the court system had already given the latter strategy a try. The Massachusetts Supreme Court had issued a ruling saying that punctuation had no part in statutes. This attempt to assert that Justice ought to extend her blindness to commas and semicolons was overoptimistic, and didn't obviate any of the interpretive problems with which the law had to contend. Any remaining hope that the law could somehow escape the challenges posed by punctuation went out the window when a semicolon set about wreaking havoc up and down the Northeast Corridor in a dramatic Massachusetts court case that caused six years of controversy in courtrooms, in legislative debates, and in the streets.

IV

LOOSE WOMEN AND LIQUOR LAWS

The Semicolon Wreaks Havoc

in Boston

In late November 1900, a spat broke out in Fall River, Massachusetts. "It was an unimportant, picayune sort of a personal quarrel," the *Chicago Tribune* reported, "but it has had results of the greatest and most widespread importance." The beginning of the story sounds like the start of a cornball joke: a man walks into a bar at 11:10 P.M., sits down, and orders himself a drink. The bar owner, knowing that the man has been patronizing a rival hotel bar, decides to spite him by refusing him his drink even though other patrons are still being served. Like any perfectly reasonable American denied a cocktail, the patron threatens to sue; and on the following day he makes good on his threat by retaining the services of a lawyer. "The lawyer brushed the dust off of [an] old statute, and there he found the semicolon—a dangerous, disastrous semicolon that would have been absolutely harmless, so far as the purposes of the wrangling Fall River citizen had been concerned, if only it had been a comma, which it wasn't."

The statute the lawyer uncovered read: "That no sale of spirituous or intoxicating liquor shall be made between the hours of 11 at night and 6 in the morning; nor during the Lord's day, except that if the licensee is also licensed as an Innholder he may supply such liquor to guests who have resorted to his house for food and lodging." Pointing to the part of the statute preceding the semicolon, the lawyer filed an injunction against the Fall River hotel bar owner to prevent him from selling between 11:00 P.M. and 6:00 A.M. A local judge granted the injunction, whereupon the bar owner appealed the decision to the Massachusetts Supreme Court.

Standing in front of the justices of the Massachusetts Supreme Court, the bar owner's lawyer argued that the semicolon in the law "was meant to be and should be construed, as a matter of fact, of being a comma"; and because the bar was situated inside a hotel, the Innholder exception should therefore apply, because if the semicolon were construed as a comma, then the clause excepting Innholders would negate *all* the rules stated in the statute. In support of his argument, the lawyer pointed out that when the law was originally passed, in 1875, it had contained a comma where the semicolon now intervened.

LAW AS ORIGINALLY PASSED	"SEMICOLONED" LAW
That no sale of spirituous or intoxicating liquor shall be made between the hours of 11 at night and 6 in the morning, nor during the Lord's day, except that if the licensee is also licensed as an Innholder he may supply such liquor to guests who have resorted to his house for food and lodging.	That no sale of spirituous or intoxicating liquor shall be made between the hours of 11 at night and 6 in the morning; nor during the Lord's day, except that if the licensee is also licensed as an Innholder he may supply such liquor to guests who have resorted to his house for food and lodging.

The original comma had been swapped to a semi-colon when several years' worth of Massachusetts statutes were consolidated into one volume in 1880. Those consolidated statutes were presented to the Massachusetts legislature in 1881 and enacted with the semicolon in place. But the 1875 parchment original of the law, the barman's attorney insisted, clearly showed a comma, making the whole debacle an error of transcription.

Some further digging revealed, however, that the transcriptionist wasn't the culprit. The consolidated version of the laws had been written by Justice Charles H. Allen, who, *The Boston Globe* observed, "seemed to take a good bit of enjoyment out of the whole matter." Allen had been transcribing from a *copy* of the original laws. Allen's copy of the laws was therefore twice removed from the original, and it turned out the semicolon had slipped in when some unknown person had created the intermediate copy from which Allen worked. But that wasn't to say that Justice Allen didn't tinker with the laws he was transcribing. The *Globe* pointed out that the transcribers openly acknowledged they had made some tweaks: "It is expressly stated . . . in the preface to the commissioners' revision of the statutes that while they have in some instances changed the phraseology, there was no intention on the part of the commissioners to change the law, but that they intended to give it as they found it."

Now it was up to the Massachusetts Supreme Court of 1900 to resolve the discrepancy between how the law had been "found" and how it was presently "given." Their task was complicated by the fact that they had two opposite precedents they could use to justify their decision. On the one hand, there was precedent for calling the punctuation in a law determinative if it could "throw light" on the meaning of the law. On the other hand, there was equal precedent for *ignoring* punctuation entirely: in an earlier ruling the court had decreed that "punctuation may be disregarded."

Years before this semicolon reared its head in Massachusetts, the U.S. Supreme Court itself had weighed in on punctuation in a case that involved not going out for bourbon, but bringing home the bacon: when some pigs escaped from a farmer's pen one night and a neighbor found and boarded them for several days, the two men got into a dispute over whether the law required the owner of the pigs to reimburse their rescuer for room and board, and a comma in the relevant statutes played a key role in the case. "The cause of all the trouble," explained *The Boston Daily Globe*, "was 10 hogs who strayed away from their comfortable, quiet sty one night, broke into the fields of literature, and became hopelessly entangled up with adverbs and commas." That court reached a conclusion that was moderate in theory, but challengingly ambiguous in practice: "Marks of punctuation may not control, but may aid in arriving at the meaning of the law."

This slippery principle was captured as best it could be in the Massachusetts liquor law decision. The Court* unanimously sided with the semicolon. The justices' first rationale for their decision was numerical: even though the original law had been passed with a comma, the revised and semicoloned law had been re-enacted repeatedly by the legislature. The semicolon had survived plenty of votes over the years, whereas the comma had only passed once. Further, the most recently published version of the statutes had given the law a title that seemed consonant with the meaning suggested by the semicolon: "An Act to prohibit the

---

* One of the justices was future Supreme Court Justice Oliver Wendell Holmes, famous for his deference to legal precedent in deciding cases.

sale of spirituous or intoxicating liquors between the hours of eleven at night and six in the morning." Here the Court once again veered away from the original version of the law, which had no such title.

Police were ordered to start enforcing the newly unearthed law immediately. Chaos descended on Boston. The public was outraged, hotel owners were outraged, and liquor distributors were outraged. Almost immediately, everyone who had an interest in the sale of booze began organizing in order to appeal to the state legislature to alter the statute on the very first day it was back in session. Accordingly, a bill to amend what had become popularly known as the "Semicolon Law" came before the Massachusetts senate in April 1901. Senator Fitzgerald of Suffolk argued in favor of the amendment, contending that "the proposition before the senate was to place the law as nearly as possible where it was when it was first enacted." But fellow Suffolk senator Mr. Howland argued that the Supreme Court had been correct in looking to the title of the statute to discern the legislature's intent, and he opposed the amendment. Senator Huntress of Middlesex, on the other hand, didn't give a damn what the intention of the legislature had been: the question was whether the proposed amendment was "better for the general welfare of the whole community" than the Semicolon Law, and he reckoned it wasn't. A vote was taken, and the amendment failed 21 to 10. The semicolon stood.

The predicament in Massachusetts began to attract national attention. A commentator for *The Washington Post*, covering the situation on the ground in Boston, wryly noted that the Semicolon Law was now "well known throughout the country, owing to the great wailing and gnashing of teeth from this Common-wealth." Bostonians weren't about to kowtow to "misfit commas and semicolons," and enterprising drinkers quickly found ways to exploit loopholes in the enforcement of the Semicolon Law. If liquor wasn't going to be sold after eleven o'clock, then why not just buy as much liquor as possible before the cutoff? There was no rule that said you couldn't go on *drinking* the booze after eleven. This attitude turned buying alcohol into a kind of competitive sport: Bostonians raced to get to restaurants as early as possible, staked out tables, and then tried to "order up the whole wine list" so that they would be adequately provisioned for the entire night. The poor souls who dared to go to the theater before dinner thus found it nearly impossible to find a seat in a restaurant after the show let out—and even if a seat *could* be found, the latecomers would have to settle for alcohol-free "temperance drinks," since by that point all the booze was sold out and making its way down the eager throats of the people who had gotten to the restaurant right at opening time.

"It is a peculiar failing of man," the *Post*'s correspondent sagely observed, ". . . that whatever is denied him, that he most earnestly desires." The threat of being unable to order alcohol after 11:00 P.M. meant that "men who at home in other cities where liquor flows like water are temperate and even abstemious—when they land in Boston after 11 o'clock are transformed into seeming dipsomaniacs. In other words, the minute they find out they cannot get a drink, they are willing to commit anything short of manslaughter to get one." Every Saturday night, the whole of New England "bore a distinct resemblance to the Fourth of July," the commentator added. Commuter trains serving the region were standing-room-only, stuffed to the gills with drunks of all descriptions. "The life of the latter-day Puritan," the *Post* concluded, "is not entirely devoid of alcoholic glee."

But this ethanol-fueled, Independence Day–style revelry was not Bacchanalian enough for opponents of the Semicolon Law, who continued to lobby fiercely for an amendment to the statute. Advocates of the law, on the other hand, pointed to the raucous behavior of Massachusetts drunks as proof positive that alcohol was a bad influence. If this was how Bostonians behaved when they had *fewer* hours of liquor-buying time, who knew to what depths they might sink if given unfettered access to alcohol? The battle between the pro– and anti–Semicolon Law camps roared vigorously on. This was great news for another punctuation mark, the exclamation point, since the Semicolon Law was "the greatest provoker of profanity yet invented."

Profane exclamations from Massachusetts citizens spurred the legislature to form a Liquor Law Committee tasked with scrutinizing the Semicolon Law. In 1904, the committee proposed a revised law that would allow innkeepers to sell alcohol until midnight, but would prevent them from going back to selling all night long, as they had done before the Semicolon Law was unearthed in the first place. This revision would mean that the statute would return to its original 1875 form, with a comma instead of a semicolon. Arguments both for and against were impassioned. "If every member of this house would vote as he drank," sniped

Representative Davis of Salem, "[the bill to repeal the Semicolon Law] would be adopted by a large majority." Nevertheless, it failed, 57–132.

The matter was far from closed, however. In February 1905, the Liquor Law Committee convened a group of "friends and foes of the semicolon" to discuss the law. For neither the first nor the last time in history, a bunch of men sat around in a room fretting that given a taste of any kind of freedom (in this case, in the form of liquor), women might ride off the rails of decency. Arguments went on all day long, and tended towards hyperbole. If "liquor dealers" were allowed one extra hour to sell booze, a Baptist minister testified, it would "cause the downfall of dozens, scores, yes, even hundreds of young women in an increased degree." The Reverend came by this opinion from having visited second-class hotels and "dance" halls—but these visits to questionable establishments, he hastened to add, were made purely from "a humanitarian standpoint."

After the minister spoke, a representative for the Massachusetts hotel association, the wine and spirit dealers' association, and the brewers' association pleaded the opposite position. "All we ask is that innholders may sell liquor to their guests one hour longer at night," the representative explained. "We don't want the semicolon law abolished, and I hope the word 'semicolon' won't be mentioned during the hearing. We're not petitioning for any change in punctuation. We simply want one hour more." One temperance advocate, B. B. Johnson, advocated instead for one hour *less*: citing a Glasgow law that had dialed back liquor hours and thereby cut down on drunkenness, he suggested liquor sales should end at 10:00 P.M., not 11:00 P.M., as the Semicolon Law specified. "Are you in favor of the sale of liquor at all?" one of the hotel association attorneys demanded, outraged by this new proposal to restrict the sale hours even more. "Only when it is needed as an antidote for disease," Johnson piously responded.

Finally, after years of fighting, the legislature passed the proposed amendment, which was then put to a popular vote on December 11, 1906. The people of Massachusetts approved. This delighted the mayor of Boston, John F. Fitzgerald,* who saw the amended stat-

---

* Mayor Fitzgerald, known as "Honey Fitz" for his smooth talking and his sweet singing voice, was future U.S. President John F. Kennedy's maternal grandfather. JFK's paternal line had an interest in liquor as well: Joseph Kennedy, JFK's father,

ute as a victory for "good sense and progressiveness" over "provincialism." Good sense or not, it was not clear that the new regulations made any real difference in the drinking habits of Massachusetts residents; the *New York Sun* snickered that on the night the act went into effect, scarcely anyone was seen availing him- or herself of the extra hour of drinking time:

> At last the "lid" was lifted. Boston was to be "gay." New York and the devil were no longer to have all the fun. . . . Dionysus, ever young and fair, was to come out of the Art museum and ride tigerback through the restaurants. . . . The home of thought was to be the palace of sport . . . . [But] Bostonians are happier under restraint.

---

made his fortune off distributing Scotch whisky. "Honey Fitz" Fitzgerald has a cocktail named after him—a version of the daiquiri, in a nod to his famous grandson's favorite tipple. If you want to try one out, shake up $1^1/_2$ ounces aged rum, $^3/_4$ ounces honey syrup, $^3/_4$ ounces fresh grapefruit juice, and 2 dashes of Peychaud's bitters with ice. Better make it a double if you're going directly on to the next chapter, where punctuation in the law takes a macabre turn.

Apparently the wry commentator in *The Washington Post* had been right: people liked their liquor to play hard to get. Still, even if alcohol consumption hadn't perceptibly increased after the law was amended, Massachusetts hotel owners felt they had cause to celebrate at their November 1909 banquet: former Senator W. A. Morse of Cape Cod said that when he had last attended the banquet, "members of the association were suffering from some errors of grammar in the laws of the state, but now they were not worried by either commas or semicolons."

POWER OF POINTS

Punctuation That Upset Work of Solons.

Comma or Semicolon Has Spoiled the Statutes.

Legal Decisions That Have Settled Colons.

Massachusetts and Ohio Cases Noted.

Baltimore Man Failed to Pay a Bill with a Semicolon.

V.

THE MINUTIAE
OF MERCY

The troubling questions of interpretation and intent that the Semicolon Law dredged up still haunt our justice system. Twenty-first-century legal thinking on the question of punctuation is ostensibly just an amplified version of the competing principles the Massachusetts Supreme Court weighed as it wrestled with the Semicolon Law case. "The modern Court recognizes that grammar and punctuation often clarify meaning," allows a 2010 guide to statutory interpretation. Yet in determining a statute's "true meaning," "the Court remains reluctant . . . to place primary importance on punctuation"—and no wonder, when there is ample precedent for invoking centuries-old English law that asserts that "punctuation is no part of a statute." Relying on this venerable principle of legal hermeneutics, the U.S. Supreme Court has ruled, for instance, that "punctuation is a most fallible standard by which to interpret a writing." Taking it even further, courts have opined that "punctuation is no part of the English language."

That latter proclamation that punctuation marks are not even part of the language you are reading right this very second seems utterly ridiculous at first but with some effort you can imagine where the idea comes from its perfectly possible to read writing with no punctuation whatsoever and understand it sure it slows you down and is pretty annoying but you damn well know what Im saying here dont you the fact is that its only in some cases that punctuation is or even could be dispositive.* Certainly when considering oral

---

* Mark Twain, famously defensive of his right to punctuate exactly how he wanted to, purportedly grew weary of criticism of his sometimes unconventional choices and published a piece of writing that was wholly without punctuation marks, but with a

testimony that has been transcribed by a court reporter, there might be grounds to disregard punctuation in attempting to figure out what was said. But even so, the guidelines I just quoted don't make much sense. For one thing, *some* punctuation marks can be considered shorthand for words. If I tell you that I want you to pick up some flour, eggs, and milk, the comma after flour pretty much means "and." It's really not clear that that comma is any different in status than a word. So everything ends up hanging on some person or persons determining what the "true meaning" of a statement is, and what kind of nebulous standard is *that* for a discipline of precision, which the law fancies itself to be?

Since it's not always easy to toss out punctuation as not "part of the English language," it's really no wonder that entire cases regularly revolve around one tiny punctuation mark. In Ohio, a woman gets out of a parking ticket because of a forgotten comma. In the

string of commas, semicolons, and other marks at the bottom of the text, along with a note telling the reader to put them where he or she pleased since Twain clearly couldn't be trusted with them. (The sources that mention this piece report it variously as a letter or as a short story; I have yet to find the Twain composition that matches this description.)

Philippines, the result of a mayoral election is voided because the court chooses to disregard a "semi-colon which the appellant views with a respect bordering on fetishism."* Cases like these are a dime a dozen. But the stakes have sometimes been much higher than traffic tickets or cocktails after 11:00 P.M. or even election results. Men have lost their lives as a result of punctuation, and it has not always been the presence of a punctuation mark but sometimes its yawning *absence* that has troubled the legal system.

A particularly heart-wrenching case that was tried on the cusp of the Great Depression painfully illustrates the problems that can be caused by a missing semicolon. In 1927, two men were convicted of murder in New Jersey. The jury's verdict and sentencing recommendation was written as follows: "We find the defendant, Salvatore Merra, guilty of murder in the first degree, and the defendant, Salvatore Rannelli, guilty of murder in the first degree and recommend life imprisonment at hard labor." The judge interpreted the life imprisonment recommendation as applicable only

---

* So much for trying to get off on a technicality!

to Rannelli, since that recommendation followed only the repetition of "guilty of murder in the first degree" after Rannelli's name. Using this reasoning, the judge sentenced Salvatore Merra to death for the same crime. In an eleventh-hour appeal, Merra's lawyer (and New Jersey senator) Alexander Simpson argued that the jury meant the life imprisonment recommendation to apply to both men—otherwise, the jurors would surely have used a semicolon to separate their verdict on Merra from their verdict on Rannelli, so that the verdict would have read: "We find the defendant, Salvatore Merra, guilty of murder in the first degree; and the defendant, Salvatore Rannelli, guilty of murder in the first degree and recommend life imprisonment at hard labor." The prosecution, on the other hand, countered that the jury clearly intended for Merra to die.

When the case was heard by the Court of Errors and Appeals of New Jersey, all but two members of the court voted to uphold the death sentence. Their votes reveal a jaw-droppingly willful blindness to facts that ought to have spared Merra. In his dissenting opinion, Justice Samuel Kalisch noted that the verdict as originally recorded at trial read: "We find the defendant Salvatore Merra guilty of murder in the first degree and the defendant Salvatore Rannelli guilty of murder in the first degree, and recommend life imprisonment at hard labor." Further, the jury was polled after the verdict and each juror repeated: "I find the defendant Salvatore Merra guilty of murder in the first degree and the defendant Salvatore Rannelli guilty of murder in the first degree and recommend life imprisonment." And the trial judge, on petition, had certified the verdict as recorded. Yet now, many months after the trial took place, the presiding judge (who had become aware of Senator Simpson's semicolon argument) suddenly insisted that the recorded verdict he had certified was "not an accurate statement of the verdict rendered by the jury," and he "rectified" the verdict by adding new punctuation and swapping a "we find" for an "and": "We find the defendant Salvatore Merra guilty of murder in the first degree. We find the defendant Salvatore Rannelli guilty of murder in the first degree, and recommend life imprisonment at hard labor." And there was even more reason than judicial shenanigans to err on the side of life imprisonment: New Jersey juries were required to make an explicit recommendation of either death or life imprisonment in first-degree murder convictions. The fact that the verdict makes explicit mention only of life imprisonment should have meant that life imprisonment was the sentence recommended for *both* men.

Kalisch's disdain for the trial judge in his dissenting opinion is clear, and the chilling conclusion he draws is worth dwelling on:

> It does not appear that the trial judge had any notes of what the verdict was and the only inference is that he must have resorted to occult means, in order to recall the intonation of the voice of the foreman of the jury, his hesitation and pauses in order to portray what took place. To countenance such interference with verdicts of a jury, especially in a case involving life, is a serious inroad on the right of trial by jury. It renders verdicts unstable and leaves a citizen accused of crime at the mercy of judicial oppression. . . . I am unwilling to consign a human being to death on any such hair splitting refinement.

Merra's appeal traveled upwards through the hierarchy of courts, finally making its way to the summer residence of United States Supreme Court Justice

Louis Brandeis. Brandeis, perched in his classic Cape house overlooking Oyster Bay River in Massachusetts, reviewed the documents but declined to grant a writ of error. Merra went to the electric chair three days after marrying the mother of his two-and-a-half-year-old son a few feet away from the death chamber. Speaking in Italian to an "unusually large" crowd gathered to watch him die—the jailhouse wedding had amplified interest in his case—he protested his innocence until the last, but to no avail. The justices up and down the court system who authorized Merra's execution had determined that the true meaning of the original verdict indicated Merra must die. What are we to make of the disturbing fact that dissenting justices found an *opposite* intelligible meaning?*

---

* The Merra decision, it is worth noting, is cited in numerous cases post-Merra. The law relies on precedent; its past is very often our present. Equally, and perhaps much more alarmingly, this is not the only punctuation-related death-penalty case in which an appeals court has lavished special powers and privileges on the trial judge. In *People v. Huggins*, a 2006 appeal case, the court examined evidence that the judge may have misinstructed the jury as to the criteria for competence to stand

Aha! you might be thinking. *So it's true what all the memes say: punctuation* is *a matter of life and death. "Let's eat grandma" really might result in somebody chowing down on a nice old lady, instead of summoning her to the Thanksgiving table as "Let's eat, grandma" would. Let's keep our commas and semicolons where the rules say they should be, and everything will be fine.* Unfortunately it isn't that simple, and the message of these cases is much darker. The moral of Merra's story is that no matter how precise you are with your punctuation, and

---

trial. The court transcript showed punctuation that differed from the standard instructions, but more seriously, it showed omission of a significant conjunction, an *and* that was critical to the meaning of the instructions. The majority opinion concludes that "it is inconceivable that the trial court misread the instruction in the nonsensical manner reflected by the punctuation supplied by the court reporter." Lone dissenter Justice Kennard pointed out how fallacious it is to assume a judge is incapable of error in such a matter, but he did so without pointing out the broader implications of this kind of decision. We should pay attention to those broader implications: what does it mean for our jury system and for our democracy that a trial judge is deferred to over a jury, or over the available evidence? See People v. Huggins 175 38 Cal.4th 175; 41 Cal.Rptr.3d 593; 131 P.3d 995 [Apr. 2006].

no matter how carefully constructed the legal rules for punctuation use and interpretation might be, there will almost always be a way to cast doubt on the origins of a punctuation mark, or on its original intended meaning, or on its most valid construction given its context. A zealous attorney might well be able to find a way to make "Let's eat, grandma" justify sticking a fork in her, particularly if the judge and jury already lean cannibal.

Bias matters, and it matters more than most of us would like to believe it does when it comes to institutions we're supposed to trust, like our legal system. Salvatore Merra, for instance, and his convicted codefendant, Salvatore Rannelli, had found themselves on trial at perhaps the worst possible time. Their original trial took place in 1926, and their appeal in the spring and early summer of 1927. The two men, Italian immigrants, were accused of murdering a paymaster in the course of a robbery. Their convictions for that crime took place in the shadow of one of the twentieth century's most notorious cases: the trial and conviction of Nicola Sacco and Bartolomeo Vanzetti. Sacco and Vanzetti were also Italian immigrants. They were also accused of murdering a paymaster in the course of a robbery.* The jury had convicted Sacco and Vanzetti after just a few hours' deliberation, but irregularities in the trial prompted appeals and protests from people around the globe urging that the verdict be overturned. Sacco and Vanzetti's supporters were fighting against intense anti-Italian and anti-immigrant sentiment. The governor of Massachusetts formed a committee to consider executive clemency for the two convicted men. The clemency committee was headed by then-president of Harvard University Abbott Lawrence Lowell, whose career highlights included a stint as an official of the Immigration Restriction League, and the enforcement of segregation on the Harvard campus. When the Lowell Committee, which deliberated behind closed doors, emerged to declare that the trial had been fair after all, journalist Heywood Broun remarked with wry wrath, "What more can two im-

---

* Sacco and Vanzetti were anarchists as well, which didn't help them one bit. The presiding judge referred to them as "anarchistic bastards." See Eric Foner, "Sacco and Vanzetti," *The Nation*, August 20, 1977, p. 137.

migrants from Italy expect? It is not every prisoner who has a president of Harvard throw on the switch for him."

Was Salvatore Merra's fate in part a product of those same prejudices of the time? It's tempting to ask, too, if the enforcement of the Semicolon Law had something to do with anti-Irish sentiments in Massachusetts, where the Irish were stereotyped as (among other things) drunks. (Think of the phrase *paddy wagon*.) The owner of the bar in Fall River who was sued for selling after 11:00 P.M. had the surname Kelley. Of course, that doesn't necessarily mean he was of Irish extraction, and even if he was, it doesn't necessarily mean that the decision of the court was motivated by bigotry. It could be coincidence. But such coincidences deserve our attention and our vigilance. So many discrete racist or otherwise malignantly biased acts can be excused as meaningless matters of happenstance, just as a puzzle piece looks like an abstract blob of nothing until hundreds of them are assembled all together and then suddenly—we see.

In one of Shakespeare's most famous scenes, which forms the climax of *The Merchant of Venice*, the beautiful Portia dresses up in drag[*] to appear in court posing as a lawyer in an attempt to save her husband's friend Antonio. Portia's husband, Bassanio, has defaulted on a loan from Jewish merchant Shylock, and as guarantor for the loan, Antonio must pay the price: per their contract, Shylock may take from him a pound of flesh. Appealing to Shylock, Portia makes a lofty plea. "The quality of mercy is not strained," she begins. "It droppeth as the gentle rain from heaven upon the place beneath." She goes on in this vein, singing the praises of mercy, and finally asking Shylock to be merciful. "I want the law," Shylock replies, resolute. And so Portia gives him the law: the terms of the contract specify that if Bassanio were to default, Shylock may collect a pound of flesh from Antonio. But, Portia cautions, the amount specified is exact. Shylock may take no more and no less than a pound, and he may take only flesh, not blood: is he certain he can be so accurate? Portia reminds him of the consequences should he err. "If the

---

[*] In the 2004 film of the play, she is wearing the type of facial hair that the newspaper reporter at the beginning of Chapter Four described as a semicolon.

scale do turn, But in the estimation of a hair, Thou diest and all thy goods are confiscate." Shylock, defeated, relents. In *The Merchant of Venice*, it isn't a pie-in-the-sky ideal of mercy that tips figurative scales of justice, but the threat of real flesh tipping real metal scales that determines the outcome of the trial. If there is mercy in the outcome for Antonio, it is an incidental by-product of precision.

The Merchant of Venice, although fiction, illustrates a fundamental truth of the law: it turns on technicality and precision. To some degree, it *must*: if the law is intended to be accessible to the people to whom it accords freedoms and restrictions, those people ought to be able to understand it clearly. But no matter how technically precise and careful, the law will always be subject to interpretation. It is often the case that more than one interpretation of the letter of the law is available to us, so that justices disposed to keep bars open or close them down could both find a rationale for doing so. The same was true of the justices disposed to save or kill Salvatore Merra. And does anyone imagine, in an alternate *Merchant of Venice* in which the debtor was the Jew and the lender a Christian, that the pound of flesh wouldn't have been paid in Shakespeare's era?

Perhaps in such an alternate version of the play, there would be mutterings from the bench about the "spirit" or "original intent"* of the contract Bassanio, Antonio,

---

* "Original intent" or "meaning" is a concept beloved of legal formalists. Legal formalism is perhaps best known to Americans through the judicial opinions of the late Supreme Court Justice Antonin Scalia, who believed that the U.S. Constitution should be applied with reference to its writers' intentions. Punctuation is taken very seriously by advocates of formalism who "accord primacy to the text, structure, and history of the document in ascertaining the meaning of its provisions and then applying that meaning in a rigorous, logically formal way." These formalists, despite their high tolerance for the "cumbersomeness" of their enterprise, do reach a limit beyond which they do not historicize further: they are willing to assume that rules and definitions accurately reflect usage, and that everyone involved in writing and publishing laws obeyed popular rule systems. As we've already seen, there's absolutely no historical grounds for those assumptions.

The summary of formalism above is a quotation from an article by two scholars who applied a strict legal formalist reading of the Constitution to Article IV, Section III, which contains a semicolon that could be interpreted to mean West Virginia, Kentucky, and Maine are unconstitutional. The authors, who rescue the three potentially unconstitutional States from oblivion in their conclusion, write that it is necessary to consult treatises on punctuation written during the time the law was composed. They come to the rather curious conclusion that "the meaning of the semicolon has not changed appreciably

and Shylock entered into. To imagine that the law is safe from the biases of one's time—be they the prejudices of sixteenth-century Venice, or twentieth-century New Jersey, or in our courtrooms today—is a dangerous dream.

The law is skeletal, a mere naked framework of words, and those words require interpretation for the law to become animate and to act in the world. Any time interpretation is involved (which really means: any time a human being gets involved in *anything*), there is the opportunity for our best and most beautiful qualities to inflect the material we are interpreting—but there is equally the opportunity for our cynicism, our racism, and our little hatreds and bigotries to be exercised through the application of laws that are at

---

in the last 213 years"—which might come as a surprise to readers accustomed to looking at either rules *or* usage from that era. Since the authors get that crucial bit of historical detail wrong, maybe West Virginia, Kentucky, and Maine don't exist after all! See Vasan Kesavan and Michael Stokes Paulsen, "Is West Virginia Unconstitutional?" *California Law Review* vol. 90, no. 2 (March 2002): 396. See also Justice Antonin Scalia's dissent in Tennessee, Petitioner v. George Lane et al., 541 U.S. 509 (2004), for a characteristic example of Scalia's use of historical dictionaries to justify an interpretation of the law.

the end of the day inert tools that must be wielded by someone to construct a more or less merciful world. Any other vision of our laws—any vision in which they are perfect and complete and speak for themselves—is fantasy. In most cases, perhaps all cases, there will be an opportunity to act ungenerously, and to let some Salvatore Merra go to the chair, or instead to take the opportunity to choose a more merciful path. Given this reality, there is no easy answer to questions of interpretation in the law, and statutory guidebooks that tell us the "rules of legal hermeneutics" will find that those interpretive rules, much like the rules of grammar books, quickly meet challenges from the complex irreducibilities of the real world. Perhaps the only thing that can be advised is that anyone charged with application of the law—a judge, a juror, a lawyer—should be always encouraging the better angels of our nature, and constantly on the lookout for the worse devils in it.

VI

CARVING SEMICOLONS IN STONE

What has been the fate of the semicolon, breaker of Bostonian spirits, and the rules that aimed to bring it to heel? In the same year the Massachusetts Semicolon Law was repealed, 1906, the Chicago Press published a two-hundred-page style guide called *Manual of Style*. Unlike the grammar textbooks of the nineteenth century, this book was not for schoolchildren, but for authors, editors, and proofreaders. Shift in audience notwithstanding, the *Manual* inherited both the nineteenth century's predilection for rules, and its worries about trends. As the *Manual* put it, "Rules and regulations such as these, in the nature of the case, cannot be endowed with the fixity of rock-ribbed law. They are meant for the average case, and must be applied with a certain degree of elasticity." The *Manual* presented its rules in numbered form, with nineteen regulations given for the most commonly used punctuation mark, the comma.

The disclaimer about "elasticity" was still being repeated over a century later in the sixteenth iteration of the *Manual*. It had "become a maxim," and was enshrined in the preface of every edition of the *Manual*.* But the rest of the book had changed considerably since it was first printed, with its major revisions pushing it farther and farther along the course initially plotted by those nineteenth-century rule setters. In the thirteenth edition, published in 1982, *A Manual of*

---

* There is now a seventeenth edition of the *Manual* (1144 pages, 40 comma rules), but its preface is almost exclusively taken up with reflections on changes necessitated by new writing and reading technologies, such as digital publishing and social media. At the end of the preface, however, the editors take care to mention that the seventeenth edition is still guided "by the principles that have been handed down through earlier editions." Presumably "elasticity" remains among them.

Style became *The Chicago Manual of Style*, which was "what everybody else calls it," and an apt reflection of the authority the book had achieved by dominating the market for stylebooks. With the definite article came a shift towards greater definitiveness all around: this was "much more a 'how-to' book for authors and editors than was its predecessor." Still, the *Manual* at least paid some lip service to taste: "Punctuation should be governed by its function, which is to make the author's meaning clear, to promote ease of reading, and in varying degrees to contribute to the author's style." There was no indication of *how* punctuation might contribute to style, and writers were warned that rules should be followed to regulate the presence of "the subjective element."

The sixteenth edition of the *Manual* (1026 pages, 37 comma rules) carried these principles still farther away from that "subjective element": the preface announced that the book would "recommend a single rule for a given stylistic matter rather than presenting multiple options." Exceptions were eliminated where possible. This was what the *Manual*'s users wanted, though it's unclear whether firmer and more numerous rules really reduced uncertainty, if *The Chicago*

Manual of Style's popular "Chicago Style Q&A" web page is any indication. On the site, anyone can write in with questions about how the rules are to be applied, and learn that if the *Manual* hasn't got the exact construction they are looking for, they can "extrapolate" from the rules that are given. Meanwhile, in the pages of the current edition of the *Manual*, authorial "style" has disappeared entirely from the punctuation section; instead, the punctuation rules the *Manual* gives are celebrated as the "logical application of traditional practice." Has *The Manual of Style* lost its sense of style?

Whether it's the *Manual* that peers down from your bookshelf, or Strunk and White, or the APA style guide, or Fowler, or Lynne Truss, it's fair to ask why we consider these books authoritative, and if there might not be some better way to assess our writing than through their dicta. It seems that stylebooks in any language aren't successfully clearing up ambiguities: Harun Küçük, a professor at the University of Pennsylvania, tells me that the semicolon is used in Turkish and Arabic too, and that writers in those languages aren't any less confused about its usage than writers in English are. Other people grope for something better than what's offered in style guides; over dinner in Berlin, my friends James Harker and Paul Festa decide that the semicolon is "the California stop of punctuation." Still others obviate the question of semicolon usage entirely: Tim Casey, an abstract painter and writer who grew up in the Southwest, tells me that "in Texas they (we) use the term 'Golly' as a universal form of punctuated pause within the clause." I don't know if I could get along solely on *Golly*s, but as I stare down bookshelves bowed under the weight of umpteen conflicting and competing style guides golly is it tempting to give it a try.

VII

SEMICOLON SAVANTS

Humorist Mark Twain wasn't averse to a "golly" or two in some of the dialogue in his books, but for anyone who dared to interfere with his punctuation, he had stronger words. "The damned half-developed foetus!" Twain raged to his U.K. publishers Chatto & Windus. Once again, Twain was excoriating a proof-reader, a professional figure who frequently met with his wrath. Ninety percent of the "labor & vexation" of writing, Twain insisted, "consists in annihilating their ignorant & purposeless punctuation & restoring my own." Affronted by the meddling proofreader, Twain noted that his punctuation was "none of [the proof-reader's] business," and reminded his publishers that he "knows more about punctuation in two minutes than any damned bastard of a proof-reader can learn in two centuries." Having satisfied himself that he'd made his point, Twain decided to conserve the rest of his vitriol for another occasion. "But this is the Sabbath Day," he closed, "& I must not continue in this worldly vein." The Sabbath cast a short shadow, however; Twain never went long without a dig at the people fussing with his grammar: "Yesterday Mr. Hall wrote that the printer's proof-reader was improving my punctuation for me," he wrote in another letter, "& I telegraphed orders to have him shot without giving him time to pray."

Twain was aggressive in his criticisms of his proof-readers because he was tuned in to the value of good punctuation.* By "good," I don't mean what rule books

---

* In fact, his punctuation was "the one thing I am inflexibly particular about. . . . It's got more real variety about it than any other accomplishment I possess, & I reverence it accordingly." Mark Twain, *Autobiography of Mark Twain, Volume 1: The Complete and Authoritative Edition*, ed. Harriet E. Smith, Benjamin Griffin, Victor Fischer, and Michael Barry Frank (Oakland: University of California Press, 2010), p. 677.

mean by "good punctuation." I mean punctuation that is effective, punctuation that is actively making a text better, punctuation that is fit to the tone and style of the text and its purpose. These criteria don't mean that good punctuation won't ever appear to play by The Rules—they just mean it's coincidental if it happens to do so. Punctuation has to be judged by how it shapes the text in which it's situated. The problem, for writers and readers, is how to go about figuring out whether punctuation is any good or not without the security of a book of rules. It's a tough thing to do, to learn to let go of getting answers from stylebooks and to replace that practice with asking exploratory questions about our texts.

I've spent a lot of years talking about punctuation—its history and its modern practices—with people who consider themselves language Learners (often students), and also with people who consider themselves language Masters (usually people who've written a few articles, or a book, or a dissertation). I've found that the Masters are the people who are most resistant to the demonstrable truths about rules (the truths you've been reading in this book). The Masters are the people who usually don't really need to refer to the rules in order to use them, and in fact they never needed to memorize the rules in the first place in order to deploy "proper English." But they're very certain, nonetheless, that rules are a good thing. These rule lovers possess an innate understanding of the proscriptions provided by rules; they like rules because the rules give words to, and validate, an instinctive understanding of usage that the rule lover already has. Perhaps this rule lover has had to memorize a few of the more obscure precepts to possess the complete set in his or her head, but the basics have been there from childhood.

I know this character well, because I *was* that rule lover, that Master. From a young age I could recite *Chicago Manual of Style* precepts by chapter and verse. I got embarrassingly loud hiccups on a school field trip when I was twelve years old because poor grammar on a sign at a national park* offended and shocked my constitution on such a visceral level. I could hear the crack of an infinitive splitting from miles off. Why, *yes,* dear college classmate, I would be *delighted* to proofread that paper for you and hand it back red.

---

* An errant apostrophe making an *its* into an *it's*.

I skipped smugly along in this fashion, straight up until I taught my first class of college students, when I was twenty-three. As soon as I was on the other side of the seminar table standing at a chalkboard, my gleeful grammar-nerdery crashed headfirst into a pretty serious pedagogical problem: rules, even when explained very carefully and consistently, didn't seem to be a good way to teach students what they wanted to know, which was how to have *control and mastery* over language. How do you make words do what you want them to? Rules couldn't answer that question.

Deep down, I think most rule lovers know this. I have yet to meet a rule lover who's been able to tell me that he or she actually learned good English usage by memorizing or consulting rules. And even if memorizing rules were a good way to learn English successfully, where would knowing and using all the rules with precision actually get you? You could write perfectly "correct" English all day and still not have what most of us *really* want, which is style. We want our words to have impact. We want our boss to implement that great new idea, we want our texts to inspire love and our tweets to get laughs, we want the eulogy to do justice, we want to sound breezy and cool in that social media profile, we want the A on the paper, we want to persuade and to be understood. Following the rules will not be sufficient to accomplish these things; some of these abilities elude even the people who consider themselves Masters. Maybe the Masters can speak "standard English" and maybe they can write well enough in obscure jargon and byzantine syntax to be published in some niche academic field, but that might be the *only* English they can speak—and that is a limitation and liability. So what if you know the password to get into the Ivory Tower if you can't get back out of it when you need some fresh air and open sky?

So we need another tactic, whether we think we consider ourselves beginners or advanced. How do we learn to use English in a way that *sticks* better and *works* better than an abstracted list of memorized rules? And how do we learn to develop a writing style that's recognizable, and at the same time master the ability to be flexible with that style as the occasion requires?

I would love to give you a quick fix for this problem. If I could give you a quick fix, I could sell a zillion copies of this book the way that a new diet book promising quick and easy weight loss sells in January. But the results of a quick-fix way to master English would be about as lasting as those of a fad diet. The truth is, it takes more work and more time to become a good English writer than anyone really wants to believe. To write well, you have to read a lot, and you have to read with attention, which is what these next sections will model. You're going to see me stop* and think, *Why did the author choose a semicolon here when she could have chosen a period?* In some cases, I'm going to look at sentences as parts of paragraphs, which are parts of chapters, which are parts of books: how does this sentence interact

---

* It can be hard to slow ourselves down and really contemplate a piece of text. That's probably always been true, but for me, at least, typing has made it more difficult; when most of my writing is done with my fingers flying over a keyboard, I can transcribe an author's words faster than my brain can properly take them in. If I really want to discipline myself and look closely at a writer's style, I still copy out sections of that author's work by hand, pen on paper. I'm a firm believer that this is the best and most reliable way to learn to be a better stylist, not just when it comes to punctuation but for the other elements of style as well. I believe this because I've seen it work, over and over, throughout the years. I recommend this technique to anyone who considers themself a student of language, no matter what age and ability.

with the sentences around it, and how does it create character in fiction or advance an idea or feeling in nonfiction? In other cases, I'll think about the author's overall style or voice or themes: how is the semicolon contributing? Here there will be no contextless "example sentences" floating in the void. Thinking that you can understand a semicolon by looking at one in a lone example sentence is like thinking you've really seen a lion because you saw one at the local zoo all alone in an enclosure chomping on a T-bone the zookeeper tossed in.

Many of the writers I'll talk about in the following sections have firm opinions about punctuation, or at least they wouldn't disavow punctuation as part of what gives their writing style. Irvine Welsh, however—one of the authors I'll touch on—might not be too impressed with my scrutiny of his semicolons:

> I use [the semicolon]. I've no feelings about it—it's just there. People actually get worked up about that kind of thing, do they? I don't fucking believe it. They should get a fucking life or a proper job. They've got too much time on their hands, to think about nonsense.

Well, them's the breaks if you're a writer. There's an extent to which your analysis of your own work is an interesting jumping-off point for criticism, but there's equally an extent to which your writing is its own entity and exists independent of you and your intentions and your hopes and dreams. Plus, it's entirely possible that a text might have its punctuation altered by a sloppy (or malicious) copyeditor; as we've seen in the chapters on the law, transcription and typesetting are vulnerable to human error. Samuel Taylor Coleridge lavished praise on the literary mastery displayed by Daniel Defoe for his use of a semicolon in *Robinson Crusoe*—a semicolon which, it turns out, doesn't appear in the majority of editions of the book. "In effect," one critic summed up, "Coleridge has chosen to praise the work of a typesetter contemporary to himself, not Defoe." So in terms of exegesis of a book, there are a lot of unknowns that render it hard to make claims about what an author's intentions really were. Even without certainty about who did what to which part of a text, we can learn by thinking carefully about punctuation in texts. Welsh can claim indeliberate semicoloning all he wants. It doesn't make it less interesting or productive to look at how the semicolon creates narrative voice and meaning in *Trainspotting*.*

THE BIG PAUSE

When we first meet private detective Philip Marlowe in Raymond Chandler's *The Big Sleep*, he is thirty-eight years old and has already seen it all. Marlowe is the consummate noir detective, so hard-boiled that even Diogenes the Cynic might have told him to chill out. In the seven novels and handful of short stories that Chandler wrote featuring Marlowe, semicolons are rare. Often, the world as Marlowe describes it tumbles forth with barely any punctuation at all: "I shaved and showered and dressed and got my raincoat out and went downstairs and looked out of the front door." Forget the semicolon, we're not even getting *commas*.

A semicolon requires effort and thought to deploy, and as we've seen, some writers avoid them entirely. So you might think, *Maybe Chandler just didn't like the*

---

* Welsh is wrong that thinking about punctuation is "nonsense," but of course he might nevertheless be right that I need to get a fucking life and a proper job.

Ralph Crane/The LIFE Images Collection/Getty Images

semicolon, or maybe he didn't know how to use one. But Chandler's essays, sparkling yet far less well-known than the Marlowe novels for which he's famous, show otherwise; the essays positively bristle with well-used semicolons. Moreover, Chandler was persnickety about syntax in general, and he wasn't afraid to growl at copyeditors who trod too close to what he considered *his* territory. Sitting at his typewriter in January 1947, peering through his horn-rimmed glasses and puffing on his pipe—at least, this is how I picture the scene, because you rarely see a photo of Chandler without a pipe jammed between his lips and a glint in his eye—he fired off a salty letter to his editor at *The Atlantic*, Edward Weeks. "By the way," Chandler spat at the end of the letter,

> would you convey my compliments to the purist who reads your proofs and tell him or her that I write in a sort of broken-down patois which is something like the way a Swiss waiter talks, and that when I split an infinitive, God damn it, I split it so it will stay split, and when I interrupt the velvety smoothness of my more or less literate syntax with a few sudden words of barroom vernacular, this is done with the eyes wide open and the mind relaxed but attentive. The method may not be perfect, but it is all I have. I think your proofreader is kindly attempting to steady me on my feet, but much as I appreciate the solicitude, I am really able to steer a fairly clear course, provided I get both sidewalks and the street between.

The Atlantic's proofreader, Margaret Mutch, got Chandler's message and wrote him a letter back. This time Chandler responded with a poem, "Lines to a

Lady with an Unsplit Infinitive," in which he imagines confronting Mutch over her correctives. The poem culminates in Mutch murdering Chandler with a crutch:

> His face was white with sudden fright,
> And his syntax lily-livered.
>
> "O dear Miss Mutch, leave down your crutch!"
> He cried in thoughtless terror.
>
> Short shrift she gave. Above his grave:
> HERE LIES A PRINTER'S ERROR.

"Roll on, roll on, thou semicolon," exhorts Chandler in one line of his impish little poem. And Chandler certainly knew how to let semicolons roll. The *Atlantic* article that prompted his letter and poem was a piece called "Oscar Night in Hollywood." There are semicolons aplenty in it, and it has two examples of one of Chandler's most characteristic uses of the semicolon: he loved to pound out a paragraph in which he dressed down someone or something in a series of clauses with more or less identical grammatical form.

If you can go past those awful idiot faces on the bleachers outside the theater without a sense of the collapse of the human intelligence; if you can stand the hailstorm of flash bulbs popping at the poor patient actors who, like kings and queens, have never the right to look bored; if you can glance out over this gathered assemblage of what is supposed to be the elite of Hollywood and say to yourself without a sinking feeling, "In these hands lie the destinies of the only original art the modern world has conceived"; if you can laugh, and you probably will, at the cast-off jokes from the comedians on the stage, stuff that wasn't good enough to use on their radio shows; if you can stand the fake sentimentality and the platitudes of the officials and the mincing elocution of the glamour queens (you ought to hear them with four martinis down the hatch); if you can do all these things with grace and pleasure, and not have a wild and forsaken horror at the thought that most of these people actually take this shoddy performance seriously; and if you can then go out into the night to see half the police force of Los Angeles gathered to protect the golden ones from the mob in the free seats but not from that awful moaning sound they give out, like destiny whistling through a hollow shell; if you can do all these things and still feel next morning that the picture business is worth the attention of one single intelligent, artistic mind, then in the picture business you certainly belong, because this sort of vulgarity is part of its inevitable price.

The semicolon can be very effective in a paragraph-long sentence like this, where it can highlight and amplify parallel structure. All those clauses in Chandler's list, which begin in the same way ("if you . . ."), sound like the authoritative repetition of a judge in a courtroom, the semicolon slamming down like a gavel between each indictment and its successor. Here Chandler created a steadiness of rhythm in his prose so that its structure and the words within it work seamlessly to create meaning.*

---

* Possibly this paragraph is also a sly world-weary riff on Rudyard Kipling's inspirational poem "If," although one would have to ask Chandler to know for sure.

Rhythm is everything for Chandler. Consider one of his other uses of the semicolon in the same "Oscar Night" essay:

> They insist upon judging it by the picture they saw last week or yesterday; which is even more absurd (in view of the sheer quantity of production) than to judge literature by last week's bestsellers, or the dramatic art by even the best of the current Broadway hits.

Punctuation can let a sentence run or it can hold it in check. Either way the effect can be thrilling. Watch the videos of the great racehorse Secretariat competing for the Triple Crown in 1973. In the Belmont Stakes you see him set free to run seemingly unchecked by his jockey: almost from the first moment of the race it is just Secretariat, Secretariat, Secretariat. He accelerates and accelerates, pulling away until there is only him in the frame when he crosses the finish line. But in the Kentucky Derby, he is held back for most of the race. For a long while he barely figures in the race caller's list of positions. Then suddenly he is let go and is away so quickly and effortlessly he appears to float. Chandler's

sentence just quoted is Kentucky Derby–style Secretariat: Chandler reins in that first clause nice and tight
and short; and then he lets it go leaping forward, surging
with energy and passion felt all the more keenly for the
compactness of that first clause. There is a moment of
transition between restraint and license to run, and that
moment is made and marked by the semicolon.[*]

Reading Chandler's essays, there can be no doubt
that he knew how to use a semicolon and *relished* using them, given their relative frequency in his nonfiction. So why is it that his fiction might contain one
or two semicolons, if any at all?[†] The key, as I hinted
at the start of this section, lies in Marlowe's character.
Marlowe rarely allows himself either the kind of re-
flective pause or the uncertainty that a semicolon permits. Marlowe knows what's what. He meets a person
and within moments has usually drawn a bead on their
innermost self. He's good at chess; he can see clearly

---

[*] In the late 1800s, incidentally, a racehorse *named* Semicolon did
exceptionally well in the major U.S. races, but he began to tire
around the turn of the century—much like the semicolon itself.

[†] I count two in *The Big Sleep*, for instance, and one in *The High
Window*.

ahead several moves. He is unmoved by the blond hair and sweet smiles of countless femmes fatales. If he makes a mistake, he doesn't spend much (if any) time on self-castigation. And perhaps most Marlowe of all is the practice of keeping his cards close to his chest. He is forever getting the players in his investigations drunk and confessional, while confessing nothing himself. Certainly a lot goes on in Marlowe's mind, but Marlowe's mind is quicksilver, all action, few pauses—often there's not even enough time for a comma.

So it is a surprise when Marlowe has a moment of vulnerability midway through *The Big Sleep*.

> I didn't mind what she called me, what anybody called me. But this was the room I had to live in. It was all I had in the way of a home. In it was everything that was mine, that had any association for me, any past, anything that took the place of a family. Not much; a few books, pictures, radio, chessmen, old letters, stuff like that. Nothing. Such as they were they had all my memories.

It is a poignant moment. Marlowe reflects on how tenuous is his sense of having any kind of home whatsoever. What takes the place of a family is "not much" and a short silence. The semicolon reads as Marlowe having to stop to think, perhaps being *made* to stop to think by his sense of loss. For once he seems unguarded. That semicolon could have been a colon or a full stop, but Chandler chose this moment to drop in one of the Marlowe books' rare semicolons.

Both this vulnerable semicolon and the racehorse semicolon we looked at prior to it are "illegal." A semicolon, *The Chicago Manual of Style* opines, is to be used either when the items in a list are lengthy and have their own internal punctuation, or when separating two independent or coordinating clauses. Neither criterion applies here. "Which is even more absurd (in view of the sheer quantity of production) than to judge literature by last week's best-sellers, or the dramatic art by even the best of the current Broadway hits" is not an independent clause. Nor does it contain so elaborate a series of punctuation of its own that it could not have been cordoned off with another punctuation mark. The same is true of "a few books, pictures, radio, chessmen, old letters, stuff like that."

If you think of Chandler's deployment of these semicolons as "breaking the rules"; if your first reaction is "Where the hell is the rest of the sentence?"; if you want to take out your red pen and start correcting; then you have missed the opportunity to feel something more meaningful than irritation. I remember watching those videos of Secretariat's races for the first time as a child. My father had given me a copy of William Nack's book *Secretariat*, and I wanted to see for myself the greatness described in its pages. In the Derby, when Secretariat was at last set free in the final stretch, I leapt to my feet and shouted. Watching the Belmont Stakes, a chill passed through my body to see such sublime athleticism let loose. Even though those races were run six years before I was born, I had the sense of something alive and unfolding, of momentum and power masterfully reserved and then unfurled, and my reaction to watching them again today, some thirty years later, is the same. Good punctuation, whether it reins in or lets go, can produce the same kinds of exhilarating effects if we aren't unwisely reined in ourselves by a sense that language is somehow obliged to a set of rules.

Lynne Truss, our wittiest contemporary rule advocate, cheekily warns that "weak-charactered writers will be encouraged to ignore the rule that only full sentences should be joined by the semicolon." Were Truss able to tease Chandler about his "weak-charactered" writing, I'd like to see what poetry might result from a face-off between the midcentury master of syntax and the modern maven of rules. But Chandler died in 1959. Beneath his name and the dates of his life, his gravestone in San Diego's Mount Hope Cemetery says nothing about a printer's error. It reads, simply, "Author."

HEROIN ADDICTS
EXPLAIN THINGS TO ME

Are semicolons always pauses, then? Moments of silence? Definitely not. There are other ways to think about the possibilities the semicolon offers a writer. To see some more semicolon tricks, it'll help to look at two writers who don't seem like they belong together in a sentence, or any other confined space: the essayist Rebecca Solnit, and the novelist Irvine Welsh. Solnit's prose is all about clarity, precision, and penetrating intellect, while Welsh spews profanity-laced Scots-English in novels like *Trainspotting*, written in the voices of a group of heroin addicts. Radically different in styles, genre, and substance though they may be, Solnit's and Welsh's prose offer an antidote to seeing a semicolon only as a pause longer than a comma or as a precise logical signifier, which are the two most frequently deployed characterizations of the semicolon that you're likely to find. A semicolon is sometimes not a pause, but the opposite: an instrument of quickness, a little springboard that launches you rapidly from thought to thought.

Trainspotting has one of these springy little semicolons in its very first sentence:

> The sweat wis lashing oafay Sick Boy; he wis trembling. Ah wis jist sitting thair, focusing oan the telly, tryin no tae notice the cunt. He wis bringing me doon. Ah tried tae keep ma attention oan the Jean-Claude Van Damme video.

This amplification to the news that Sick Boy was sweating, that he was also trembling, has the air of a conspiratorial addendum, the way that good gossip is often quickly whispered. Sick Boy is irritating the narrator of this chapter, Mark Renton, so he talks a little shit about him to us readers.

It's not like the semicolon was Welsh's only option. He could have squealed to a complete halt:

> The sweat wis lashing oafay Sick Boy. He wis trembling. Ah wis jist sitting thair, focusing oan the telly, tryin no tae notice the cunt. He wis bringing me doon. Ah tried tae keep ma attention oan the Jean-Claude Van Damme video.

Instead, Welsh uses the semicolon to create energy and the kind of molten realism characteristic of his caustic prose. Renton's voice has much more texture and life for having three different punctuation marks playing off one another in this paragraph than it would with only commas and periods.

It seems Welsh is fond of this strategy for opening lines, and who can blame him? For his books it works well to make his readers feel dropped into a racing river, swept into the action from the first moment. Welsh's opening paragraph in "A Soft Touch" makes use of the same type of quick semicolon: "It wis good fir a while wi Katrina, but she did wrong by me. And that's no jist something ye can forget; no jist like that."

Rebecca Solnit, too, deploys semicolons that speed

things up rather than slowing them down. In "Diary," she reflects on the changes wrought by modern technology, and reminisces about a pre-1995 world: "That bygone time had rhythm, and it had room for you to do one thing at a time; it had different parts; mornings included this, and evenings that, and a great many of us had these schedules in common." The sentence, like the day from the past that Solnit describes in it, is divided; but, like that past day, it has a flow and forward trajectory as a result of the divisions. The semicolons are responsible for both these syntactical virtues, which mirror the virtues of the "bygone time." The effect is like a stone skipping across water, lightly touching it three times, just for a split second, before hopping on. Think about how different this sentence would be if Solnit had chosen to put a colon either after *time* or after *parts*, as she very well could have. That sentence would seem comparatively heavy and academic. The quick-skip lightness of Solnit's semicolons, by contrast, has a pleasing breeziness that suits her nostalgic attitude towards the bygone time she describes.

Solnit seems to like semicolon duos and trios, and they are usually fleet-footed semicolons like the ones just quoted, but they enact a subtler kind of speeding-up as well. Have a look at these three separate semi-colon sequences, each of which fires off data supporting Solnit's central argument:

Instead, we hear that American men commit murder-suicides—at the rate of about twelve a week—because the economy is bad, though they also do it when the economy is good; or that those men in India murdered the bus rider because the poor resent the rich, while other rapes in India are explained by how the rich exploit the poor; and then there are those ever-popular explanations: mental problems and intoxicants—and for jocks, head injuries.

Of course, women are capable of all sorts of major unpleasantness, and there are violent crimes by women, but the so-called war of the sexes is extraordinarily lopsided when it comes to actual violence. Unlike the last (male) head of the International Monetary Fund, the current (female) head is not going to assault an employee at a luxury hotel; top-ranking female officers in the US military, unlike their male counterparts, are not accused of any sexual assaults; and young female athletes, unlike those male football players in Steubenville, aren't likely to urinate on unconscious boys, let alone violate them and boast about it in YouTube videos and Twitter feeds.

Good things came about with the new technologies. Many people now have voices without censorship; many of us can get in touch with other ordinary citizens directly, through every new medium, from blogs to tweets to texts to posts on FB and Instagram. In 1989, Tiananmen Square was the fax revolution. Email helped organize the Seattle WTO shutdown in 1999; Facebook was instrumental in the Arab Spring's initial phase in 2011; Occupy Wall Street was originally a Twitter hashtag.

We readers leap from fact to fact, but I would lay down a decent chunk of change that Solnit didn't. Each of these facts and figures required research, possibly even several hours of research in order to dig up a relevant statistic, verify that the methodology that produced it was sound, and survey any competing data that might challenge its veracity.[*]

A great essay is like a great nature show. Sir David Attenborough, his plummy voice suddenly sharp with excitement, narrates a dramatic chase scene on Fernandina Island in the Galápagos. Fernandina is a foreboding volcanic landscape that's home to over seven thousand seafaring marine iguanas, which can hold their breath up to half an hour as they dive and graze the sea grasses. A newly hatched marine iguana cautiously lifts his head out of the island's pebbly substrate, just enough to roll one bright little eye around his surroundings. Almost as soon as he decides it's safe to emerge, dozens of racer snakes dart from the shadows of the rocks. The iguana seems almost impossibly light on his brand-new feet, but there are too many snakes, hordes and hordes of them spilling out from under every overhang, and soon the iguana has disappeared into

---

[*] The problem is magnified in historical narrative nonfiction. The labor that can go into summoning the atmosphere of another era is boggling—a historian might spend hours poring over old newspapers to find out how hot some particular day was, just for half a sentence adding color to the past.

a greedy knot of them. The same fate befalls a second tiny iguana. And it seems a third is destined for the same gruesome end . . . but this one improbably slips free, soaring to safety on the rocks near the shore as one last racer snake flails his fangs at the iguana's heels. The entire chase sequence lasts less than six minutes. But a few minutes of what is "wild" and "natural" in these shows takes hundreds of hours of filming to achieve: the *Planet Earth* crew staked out the iguana's hatching ground dawn to dusk for two weeks to gather footage. Indeed, the hour-long "Islands" episode as a whole required three and a half years to plan, shoot, and produce—all to give us a glimpse of business as usual in the natural world.

Likewise, a really great essay puts on display the seemingly natural movement of the author's thoughts which, in reality, required supernatural effort and umpteen takes to collect and edit. "Remember that writing is not typing," Solnit advises. "Thinking, researching, contemplating, outlining, composing in your head and in sketches, maybe some typing with revisions as you go and then more revisions, emendations, additions, reflections, setting aside and returning afresh, because a good writer is always a good editor of his or her work." Reading a good essay is a bit like watching a well-edited nature show. It gives the *illusion* of thought spilling naturally and fluidly onto the page. In Solnit's case, semicolons are quick cuts keeping things exciting and saving the reader from the sense of labor and drudgery that the author herself no doubt expended.

Having managed to run the gauntlet of racer snakes, the baby marine iguana is in position to make his first dive into the sea, where he'll swim deftly through the currents to nip at a green carpet of plants. Now we, too, dive into the sea, in search of more semicolons.

BLUBBER AND BLATHER

At the time of Herman Melville's death in 1891, his novel *Moby-Dick* had sold only a few thousand copies. When the book's publishing house burned down in 1853, two years after publication, there were still first-run copies of it stacked in the warehouse, feeding the flames. Melville spent much of his working life as a customs inspector after finally throwing in the towel on writing.

No doubt the generally negative reviews that *Moby-Dick* received contributed to its floundering in bookshops. Its thick and thorny prose clambered down one page and onto the next in long paragraphs studded with every word between the covers of *Webster's*, plus a few more that Melville had invented for the book. One reviewer, having managed to slash through this thicket and come out the other side of the novel alive but not unscathed, minced no words of his own in concluding his testy review: "But if there are any of our readers who wish to find examples of bad rhetoric, involved syntax, stilted sentiment and incoherent English, we will take the liberty of recommending to them this precious volume of Mr. Melville's." He was not alone in his assessment: most reviewers seemed perplexed and frequently infuriated by Melville's elliptical, meandering prose. "The style of his tale is in places disfigured by mad (rather than bad) English," lamented a critic for the *London Athenaeum*.

Some of the book's madness undoubtedly stems from its conceit as a dodgy draft of a true story. *Moby-Dick* is told in the first person. Some (maybe most) first-person books are just told from within the narrator's perspective without being *conceptualized* as books.

Moby-Dick is different. It's presented as Ishmael's written account of his days on the *Pequod*, the whaling ship that sets out in pursuit of the infamous white whale. This book, the product of his education at sea, might prove the only good and profitable thing he's ever done.

> And, as for me, if, by any possibility, there be any as yet undiscovered prime thing in me; if I shall ever deserve any real repute in that small but high hushed world which I might not be unreasonably ambitious of; if hereafter I shall do anything that, upon the whole, a man might rather have done than to have left undone; if, at my death, my executors, or more properly my creditors, find any precious MSS. in my desk, then here I prospectively ascribe all the honour and the glory to whaling; for a whale-ship was my Yale College and my Harvard.

Not only is *Moby-Dick* self-consciously Ishmael's book, it's a *draft* of a book—at least, to the extent that Ishmael is aware how much is left necessarily unfinished in it. Near the end of his catalog of whales, he adds a little apologia:

Finally: It was stated at the outset, that this system would not be here, and at once, perfected. You cannot but plainly see that I have kept my word. But I now leave my cetological System standing thus unfinished, even as the great Cathedral of Cologne was left, with the crane still standing upon the top of the uncompleted tower. For small erections may be finished by their first architects; grand ones, true ones, ever leave the copestone to posterity. God keep me from ever completing anything. This whole book is but a draught—nay, but the draught of a draught. Oh, Time, Strength, Cash, and Patience!

At least one modern fan of *Moby-Dick* acknowledges this aspect of the text as part of its beauty and magic: "But 'Moby-Dick' is not a novel. It's barely a book at all," wrote Philip Hoare in *The New Yorker*. "It's more an act of transference, of ideas and evocations hung around the vast and unknowable shape of the whale, an extended musing on the strange meeting of human history and natural history." These "ideas and evocations" that are "hung around" the whale are held in suspension by the book's four-thousand-odd semicolons, sturdy little nails holding narrative thread spread out wide enough to comprehend not just a whale but everything the whale comes to mean to the men hunting it.

Plotwise, the book isn't really all that. "The plot is meagre beyond comparison, as the whole of the incident might very conveniently have been comprised in half of one of these three interminable volumes," complained a reviewer for the *London Britannia;* many modern readers have felt the same way.[*] The truly great moments in the book come when Ishmael goes off on what could be considered a tangent. There are entire chapters devoted to whale fat, or to the color white, or to questions about whether the whale has shrunk since God first created it. At the paragraph level, too, Ishmael is prone to wandering off.

It's true that Melville isn't afraid of a long sentence,

---

[*] One of my favorite college professors was an ex-lawyer who retained an attorney's prose sensibility when reading essays. Any superfluous or vague adjective was excised, leaving a red looping line with "DOES NO WORK" written neatly beside the wound. I sometimes imagine what *Moby-Dick* might look like if he dug into the heap of adjectives and adverbs sitting atop nearly every noun and verb.

but I've seen longer sentences. (Ask me about my Faulkner phase.) No, it's not really that Melville uses the semicolon to stretch out the distance between a capital letter and a period; instead, the semicolons are in the service of carrying you slowly, gently, pleasurably away from whatever it was you thought you were reading about—the process of beheading a whale, or how to assess winds, or cannibalism.

I say "pleasurably," but of course some people don't find these digressions pleasurable at all, and would have agreed with Melville's contemporary critics, not our present-day appraisal of the book, which counts it among the best of American novels. After it was rediscovered by literary critics in the 1920s, Melville's flop was transformed into a classic. Readers now pick it up based on its literary repute or because it's a requirement for a class, and after a few pages many of those readers would gladly hurl it into the depths. Even when the action picks up, Ishmael's narration isn't exactly economical. He often uses semicolons to string several events into sequence.

When instantly, the entire ship careens over on her side; every bolt in her starts like the nail-heads of an old house in frosty weather; she trembles, quivers, and nods her frightened mast-heads to the sky. More and more she leans over to the whale, while every gasping heave of the windlass is answered by a helping heave from the billows; till at last, a swift, startling snap is heard; with a great swash the ship rolled upward and backward from the whale, and the triumphant tackle rises into sight dragging after it the disengaged semicircular end of the first strip of blubber.

Even his *jokes* require extended setups that sometimes take the text wandering off from the matter at hand (and the matter at hand is, as always, more likely than not to be tangential to the "main events" of the book already):

In the case of a small Sperm Whale the brains are accounted a fine dish. The casket of the skull is broken into with an axe, and the two plump, whitish lobes being withdrawn (precisely resembling two large puddings), they are then mixed with flour, and cooked into a most delectable mess, in flavor somewhat resembling calf's head, which is quite a dish among some epicures; and everyone knows that some young bucks among the epicures, by continually dining upon calves' brains, by and by get to have a little brains of their own, so as to be able to tell a calf's head from their own heads; which, indeed, requires uncommon discrimination. And that is the reason why a young buck with an intelligent-looking calf's head before him, is somehow one of the saddest sights you can see. The head looks a sort of reproachfully at him, with an 'Et tu, Brute!' expression.

But wait—we were supposed to be talking about eating *whales*. . . .

"Its oceanic reach and perverse digression provide endless sources of inspiration and interpretation," writes Philip Hoare. "In chapters such as the famously sublime 'The Whiteness of the Whale'—almost hallucinatory in its associative suspension of normality and subtle obscenity—Melville takes up his theme, then takes it apart, teasing it out to impossibly filigreed tendrils, until you wonder how you, or he, got there in the first place." Eventually Melville's disquisition on the idea of whiteness winds its way back to the matter of hunting Moby-Dick, but only after sideswiping practically every subject in the arts and sciences:

> Is it that by its indefiniteness it shadows forth the heartless voids and immensities of the universe, and thus stabs us from behind with the thought of annihilation, when beholding the white depths of the milky way? Or is it, that as in essence whiteness is not so much a color as the visible absence of color, and at the same time the concrete of all colors; is it for these reasons that there is such a dumb blankness, full of meaning, in a wide landscape of snows—a colorless, all-color of atheism from which we shrink? And when we consider that other theory of the natural philosophers, that all other earthly hues—every stately or lovely emblazoning—the sweet tinges of sunset skies and woods; yea, and the gilded velvets of butterflies, and the butterfly cheeks of young girls; all these are but subtile deceits, not actually inherent in substances, but only laid on from without; so that all deified Nature absolutely paints like the harlot, whose allurements cover nothing but the charnel-house within; and

when we proceed further, and consider that the mystical cosmetic which produces every one of her hues, the great principle of light, for ever remains white or colorless in itself, and if operating without medium upon matter, would touch all objects, even tulips and roses, with its own blank tinge—pondering all this, the palsied universe lies before us a leper; and like wilful travellers in Lapland, who refuse to wear colored and coloring glasses upon their eyes, so the wretched infidel gazes himself blind at the monumental white shroud that wraps all the prospect around him. And of all these things the Albino Whale was the symbol. Wonder ye then at the fiery hunt?

The semicolon was the perfect punctuation mark for capturing the "mystical and well nigh ineffable" "horror" occasioned by the whiteness of the whale, which Ishmael "almost despair[ed] of putting in a comprehensible form."

Some readers thought Ishmael's despair was well-justified. Suggestive and beautiful though Melville's disquisition on the whale's whiteness may be to many readers (myself included), it confounded and repelled others, especially those who picked up a copy of *Moby-Dick* after devouring one of Melville's previous novels. He didn't start out his literary career with the penumbral writing style that fogged the plot of *Moby-Dick*. His first novel, *Typee*, was a bestselling account of two sailors' adventures in Polynesia. Many critics longed to return to those islands. "Mr. Melville grows wilder and more untamable with every adventure," a review in the *New York Evangelist* observed. "In *Typee* and *Omoo*, he began with a semblance of life and reality, though it was often but the faintest kind of semblance. As he advanced, he threw off the pretense of probability, and wandered into the mist and vagueness of poetry and fantasy, and now in this last venture, has reached the very limbo of eccentricity."* *Typee*, with its "semblance of reality," had less use for the semicolon (although to be sure, Melville still exercised it plenty). The novel clocked in at around 107,000 words and

---

* The reviewer meant "limbo" as in a place of oblivion, but for the modern reader more familiar with the West Indies dance, the idea of Melville bending over backwards to scoot under an ever-lowering bar of literary decency works just as well to capture this critic's opinion.

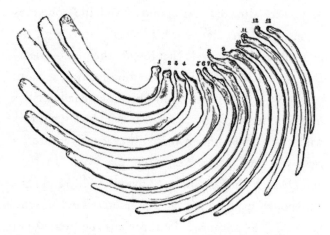

Bones of the right whale, from *Recent Memoirs on the Cetacea* (1866)

845 semicolons, a rate of approximately one semicolon for every 127 words. *Moby-Dick*, on the other hand, was about double the length at around 210,000 words, but had *4000* semicolons. That's one for every 52 words. The semicolons are *Moby-Dick*'s joints, allowing the novel the freedom of movement it needed to tour such a large and disparate collection of themes.

D. H. Lawrence, who helped dredge Melville back up from obscurity in the 1920s, wrote of *Moby-Dick* that "there is something really overwhelming in these whale-hunts, almost superhuman or inhuman, bigger than life, more terrific than human activity." In its narrative structure and ambition as well as its themes, *Moby-Dick* was ahead of its time, in uncharted waters. Just as sailors needed instruments to wander out past sight of shore, *Moby-Dick* required writing technologies that could allow it to venture out beyond the genre constraints of its time, and one of those technological marvels—as slender and significant as a compass needle—was the semicolon.

TRUST ME, I'M A WRITER

Looking at me over the rim of a teacup on a rainy London afternoon, my British friend Suzanne chooses her words carefully. "We don't really think of him as a popular writer," she says diplomatically, in response to my announcement that I'm working on a section on Henry James's semicolons. We Americans don't think of him as a popular writer either, I assure her.

If reviews for *Moby-Dick* ranged from lukewarm to cool, reviews for Henry James's later work were often ice cold. His books produced "acute periodic exasperation" in their readers. His sentences were "cumbrous and difficult, struggling through a press of hints and ideas." A review of his 1904 book, *The Golden Bowl*, appeared under the heading "A Novel for the Select Few." The reviewer wagered that "a more difficult book to read surely was never written. It is the minutest study in the psychological analysis of certain highly complex, over-refined, over-sensitised present-day persons." For casual readers, the book was "unreadable," and anyone with any kind of a life beyond sprawling on a chaise longue had better not even try: "Life is too short to master its intricacies of style and treatment." Or, as another, more circumspect reviewer tactfully put it, the book was to be recommended only for "the seasoned reader of Henry James."*

Melville, at least, was allowed to fade quietly back into an ordinary life after *Moby-Dick* bombed. Henry James had no such luck, in part because of his famous older brother, William. William James, psychologist and philosopher, was beloved by the public. He thrived

---

* Modern reader "Sandra," reviewing *The Portrait of a Lady* on Amazon UK, has an apt diagnosis to offer: "Author just likes to write, almost anything than get to the crux of the story." She gave it one star.

in front of a crowd; Henry, on the other hand, declined to give interviews and eventually holed up in quiet Sussex, England. Like so many younger brothers, Henry was destined to be compared to his older sibling whether he liked it or not. The long shadow William's accomplishments cast didn't offer much in the way of flattering lighting for Henry:

> Someone has said that "Henry James is a novelist who writes like a psychologist and William James a psychologist who writes like a novelist." The epigram pays the greater compliment to the psychologist for it is much more difficult for a man of science to write charmingly of his speciality than for a literary man to acquire mannerism and become obscure. Certain it is that William James is the most popular of philosophers and Henry James not impossibly the least popular of novelists.

In his sixties, facing down a lifetime of mixed reviews, Henry went back through his early novels and stories and created revised versions of them. These heavily altered stories were published by Scribner between

1907 and 1909 and are known as the "New York Editions." James's revisions shone harsh introspective light into previously shadowy corners of his characters' minds, exploding sentence after sentence with laborious psychological detail. The revisions are perplexing; suddenly, there is little space for the reader's imagination or inference. Every thought is so painstakingly spelled out, every object so slavishly described, that the atmosphere of the book becomes suffocating. Nothing is left unsaid.

Sentences puffed out in this way become difficult even to comprehend. Watch how the directness of a sentence in James's 1877 edition of his novel *Roderick Hudson* becomes tortured and effortful. The original version was no short sentence, but it was well-managed:

> She was a woman for the light, not for the shade; and her natural line was not picturesque reserve and mysterious melancholy, but frank, joyous, brilliant action, with just so much meditation as was necessary, and not a grain more.

Revised, its punctuation barely holds it together: phrases come rushing like water through the barriers of colons and commas and semicolons.

She was a creature for the sun and the air, for no sort of hereditary shade or equivocal gloom; and her natural line was neither imposed reserve nor mysterious melancholy, but positive life, the life of the great world—his great world—not the *grand monde* as there understood if he wasn't mistaken, which seemed squeezable into a couple of rooms of that inconvenient and ill-warmed house: all with nothing worse to brood about, when necessary, than the mystery perhaps of the happiness that would so queerly have come to her.

"You can never revise too often!" I used to tell students, before I had read much James.

One of the starkest differences generated by James's revisions can be glimpsed in a climactic scene near the end of *Portrait of a Lady*. Isabel Archer, the protagonist, has been tricked into marrying Gilbert Osmond, who schemes with his ex-lover Madam Merle to poach the extraordinary fortune Isabel has inherited. After discovering Osmond's deception, Isabel finds herself alone with an admirer she had once rejected, Caspar Goodwood. In the original 1881 edition of the novel,

James's account of what passes between Isabel and Goodwood is oblique, restrained, and allows the simile of "lightning" maximum impact. "He glared at her a moment through the dusk, and the next instant she felt his arms about her and his lips on her own lips. His kiss was like a flash of lightning; when it was dark again she was free." Why on earth did James need to tinker with this perfect set of sentences? But tinker he did.

> His kiss was like white lightning, a flash that spread, and spread again, and stayed; and it was extraordinarily as if, while she took it, she felt each thing in his hard manhood that had least pleased her, each aggressive fact of his face, his figure, his presence, justified of its intense identity and made one with this act of possession. So had she heard of those wrecked and under water following a train of images before they sink. But when darkness returned she was free.

It's not that the revision makes for an *awful* passage. It's just that compared to the original, it feels so heavy-handed. Looking at the grammar of the original version of the sentence, I picture Gale Sondergaard in the noir cinema classic *The Letter*, hovering behind a beaded curtain in a glittering dress. The semicolon is that tantalizing veil shimmering between the two halves of the sentence, showing us just enough to let us dream.

In the revised version of the passage, on the other hand, the semicolon makes me think of Sisyphus. That semicolon is a shoulder pressed against the heaviness of the back half of the sentence, trying desperately to huff its weight forwards so that . . . well, I'm not sure, exactly. But wherever James is going with the sentence, that semicolon is straining just to keep the whole thing from collapsing on itself. More significant even than the shift in style is the loss of a potently poetic irony. In the revised version, we lose the beautifully ominous paradox of the proximity of the flash of lightning, the spark of passion that traps Isabel, to the freedom that comes when that bright light is extinguished. The attraction that Isabel feels to Goodwood is a different type of constraint than her marriage to Osmond, but it is, nonetheless, a loss of freedom in which she does not act but is acted upon; when the light vanishes and she is "free," she runs.

In the passages he went back and painstakingly

altered, James's modifications feel anxious, as though he were nervous we readers just couldn't be trusted with the freedom of the first version. What might we imagine, what might we feel? Better not to leave it up to us, he seems to have decided. Not only did he bloat sentences throughout the book with a map of Isabel's every thought, he changed the ending of the novel, removing any ambiguity as to whether Isabel might reject Osmond and choose Goodwood instead, or even reject them both and strike out on her own. In the revised version, he made it as clear as he could that Isabel returned to Osmond. There is no other choice for us to consider. And so he closed the gaps, sweeping away the vague.

On the other hand, Henry's famous older brother not only allowed for vagueness, he celebrated it. "It is in short, the reinstatement of the vague and inarticulate to its proper place in our mental life which I am so anxious to press on the attention," he wrote in his magnum opus, *The Principles of Psychology*. So often we think it is the business of science always to be exact, but William James had rather the opposite idea when he set about founding the Psychology Department at

Harvard. "The boundary line of the mental is certainly vague," he urged.

> It is better not to be pedantic, but to let the science be as vague as its subject, and include such phenomena as these if by so doing we can throw any light on the main business at hand. . . . At a certain stage in the development of every science a degree of vagueness is what best consists with fertility.

William searched for ways to unfold possibility in his writing. "Use the word 'field' here for 'datum'—it is conveniently ambiguous," he corrected himself in the margins of lecture notes. He used "vague" as a compliment when evaluating psychological terminology like "idea." William's revisions opened windows; Henry's revisions slammed doors.

The semicolon, as the first version of Isabel Archer and Caspar Goodwood's kiss shows, can certainly support vagueness. Indeed, that's one of the charges leveled at it by semicolon hater Professor Paul Robinson. The semicolon, Robinson contends, is frequently "used to gloss over an imprecise thought." Semicolons, he goes on, "place two clauses in some kind of relation to one another but relieve the writer of saying exactly what that relation is."*

Poetic omissions of the type Henry James produced at his best would certainly fall into the category of "imprecise thoughts." A lot of people, not just Robinson, find an imprecise thought uncomfortable: to these types, it looks like a leak to plug rather than an opportunity to let thoughts flow. Some of those leak-pluggers end up clogging up the works professionally, by becoming analytic philosophers. The analytic philosopher (there are other types of philosophers—or, as I usually think of them, other lunch-table cliques in philosophy) thinks of himself as clear, objective, and precise, and loves to start sentences with phrases like *It*

---

* It is true that the semicolon can be used to cover up sloppy reasoning, but that scarcely seems to be a problem inherent in, or exclusive to, that particular punctuation mark. You want to see some imprecise thoughts? I can manufacture some for you, with naught but a handful of words and maybe a period. Nonetheless, these glossings-over that often accompany the semicolons Robinson encounters (he refers in particular to student papers) generate a sense of repulsion in him, and he himself eschews the mark wherever possible.

is obvious . . . or *It is clear that. . . .* Vagueness, especially *deliberate* vagueness, is apt to cause these types to hyperventilate. In spite of this, analytic philosophers consider a master of strategic vaguery, Ludwig Wittgenstein, one of their founding fathers. Wittgenstein sometimes wrote in aphorisms, and even those who claim him as part of the analytic camp admit he was "exotic" and had a writing style that "transcends the limits of academic philosophy." Occasionally, the temptation to try to iron out Wittgenstein's ambiguities and bring him in line with more status-quo philosophical writing became overwhelming for his translators, many of whom were coming from the analytic camp themselves. Check out what G. E. M. Anscombe perpetrates when she translates this fantastically vague semicolon from Wittgenstein's German into English. Here's the original:

> Der Philosoph behandelt eine Frage; wie eine Krankheit.

Which you *could* translate so as to preserve the ambiguity in it:

> The philosopher treats a question; like an illness.

But Anscombe renders it:

> The philosopher's treatment of a question is
> like the treatment of an illness.

What a different sentence that is. Gone is what German Philosophy expert Erich Heller called a "profound" semicolon, a semicolon that "marks a frontier between a thought and a triviality." Could Anscombe just not stand the uncertainty in it, and the multiple possible meanings that that uncertainty permits? I guess the analytic philosopher treats ambiguity; like an illness.[*]

Henry James, at his best, *could* stand uncertainties. So often his early writing explored what is only

---

[*] Although I'm not a fan of Anscombe's imposing her own yen for systematization and certainty on Wittgenstein here, let no one think Anscombe wasn't a badass. A dazzling and powerful thinker whose extraordinary abilities were acknowledged even in the boys' club of mid-1900s philosophy, she took no shit from anyone. Once, in Boston, she attempted to enter a formal restaurant wearing trousers. When told ladies were not allowed to enter in trousers, she simply whipped them off and walked on in. See Jane O'Grady, "Elizabeth Anscombe: An Exhilarating Philosopher, She Took to Sporting a Monocle and Smoking Cigars," *The Guardian*, January 10, 2001.

imagined or hinted at between two people. Of the first version of *Portrait of a Lady*, one of James's reviewers wrote, "As a rule Mr. James rejects symphonies, and attempts no harmonizing conclusions. He leaves us usually tantalized, half angry with an end which is left to our imagination." That was precisely his strength. Of the Tartarean options, I definitely prefer Tantalizing ambiguities to Sisyphean semicolons.

But that reviewer of James is correct that uncertainty, ambiguity, and vagueness do put a certain burden on the reader. Or maybe it's better to say: they highlight the fact that writing is an exchange between at least two people: writer and reader, or sometimes writer and the writer's own future self. There is nothing wrong with trying to be as precise as possible in your writing, or with trying to be clear; those goals are often productive and have their place. But I don't think it's such a bad thing sometimes to be engaged in the practice of working things out in words, of having a conversation. Ambiguity can be useful and productive, and it can make some room for new ideas. It can help the reader *create* something out of the materials the writer provides. As we've seen in Chapters Four and Five, even writing meant to be crystal-clear contains points that can be argued, so it's worth thinking constructively about what productive possibilities ambiguity allows and how we can tell when an ambiguity is useful rather than just pretending we can eliminate it if we only try hard enough.

Ambiguity can be so unsettling in part because when it comes down to it, all writing is an act of trust. As a reader, you trust a writer to give you some payoff for your efforts. You trust the writer to be telling you the truth, or trying. In turn, as a writer—of an email, a letter, a tweet, a book—you hope that your reader will be generous in interpreting your words. You hope you'll be taken seriously when you want to be. You hope to be understood. Trying to eliminate ambiguity (however doomed a task that is) can at least soothe that anxiety a bit. But art that allows the imagination to participate in it—the kind of art Henry James's early novels displayed—is a beautiful testament to the value that can lie in ambiguity. Uncertainty, after all, is very human, and can call forth our best human virtues. "If you only trust me, how little you'll be disappointed!" Goodwood says to Isabel, a line that James left unrevised in *Portrait of a Lady*. If only you'd trust us readers, Henry, how little you might be disappointed too.

THE LINE AND THE DASH:
WHY USE THE SEMICOLON NOW?

Perhaps because of the persistent criticism his novels faced, Henry James did not give interviews. His reticence was well-known, and so it was a surprise and delight for a journalist for *The New York Times* to be granted the opportunity to conduct James's very first interview in 1915, when he was seventy-two years old. James was prodded out of his silence by his desire to make public the charitable work of the American Volunteer Motor Ambulance Corps. Anxious to make certain his thoughts were represented properly, James spoke "with much consideration" and asked that "his punctuation as well as his words should be noted." Perhaps emboldened by James's having raised the topic himself, the interviewer broke from the designated topic of the discussion mid-interview. "Are you not famous, Mr. James," he asked, "for the use of dashes?" The response was sharp and swift.

"Dash my fame!" he impatiently replied. "And remember, please, that dogmatizing about punctuation is exactly as foolish as dogmatizing about any other form of communication with the reader. All such forms depend on the kind of thing one is doing and the kind of effect one intends to produce. Dashes, it seems almost platitudinous to say, have their particular representative virtue, their quickening face, and, to put it roughly, strike both the familiar and the empathic note, when those are the notes required, with a felicity beyond either the comma or the semicolon; although indeed a fine sense of the semicolon, like any sort of sense at all for the pluperfect tense and the subjunctive mood, on which the whole perspective in a sentence may depend, seems anything but common."

Today it's hard to imagine an author being famous for dashes, as Henry James was. In his work, the dash—cutting a path through most any page you turn to—is like a vector arrow charting the swift forward trajectory of a character's thoughts, or sometimes just the opposite—an arm outstretched as a barrier to keep one thought from tumbling into the next, so quickly do they spill out on the page. In his private letters, the dash was conscripted to signal a change of topic the way we might use a paragraph indent.—James's multipurpose use of the dash now looks remarkably modern, but he certainly didn't use it reflexively out of lack of thinking through the options, the way many of us are guilty of deploying it today. It's too bad, really: the dash can be brilliant. The electrifying German Romantic writer Heinrich von Kleist used the dash in his 1808 short story "Die Marquise von O . . ." to capture the forgotten space of time during which the unconscious Marquise is raped. It is a masterpiece of mimesis and ironic understatement. Nearly every line of Emily Dickinson's later poetry is sliced with a dash or two. Nicholson Baker was fond of a dash followed by a comma, a hybrid mark he dubbed "the dashtard." All these uses of the dash represented deliberation and careful choice.

But the dash nowadays is the Punctuation Mark of First Resort, able to take the place of commas, colons, semicolons, and periods. We now live in the Era of the Dash. Dashes are dashed off right and left by millions of thumbs sweeping fleetly across millions of mobile phones. A couple years ago I gave up using the dash for Lent[*] when I noticed a page of my writing was downright staticky with horizontal lines. I wore out my backspace key sticking to my resolution. The dash is so easy, so quick, and—when deployed in the way we often do now—so conveniently empty of meaning.

It's easy enough to blame all of this on the evils of technology, and to act as though the world is fundamentally changing, fracturing, and getting worse; in that reading of reality, the homogenizing force of the dash is a symptom of this larger decline. In convincing ourselves of this, we march backwards in the footsteps of our ancestors. Thoreau built his cabin alone on Walden Pond to "live deep" away from the buzzing city over 150 years ago. The world has always seemed too noisy and too quick. It's worth remembering that for all the things that have capsized in the wake of technological progress, there are new pleasures too: long-lost friends rediscovered through a Google search; online communities coalescing around every obscure interest imaginable; the ability to read books in completely new

---

[*]   I haven't got a religious bone in my body, but I enjoy the Lenten ritual of challenging oneself with deprivation of some kind.

ways solely through having the tools to search them efficiently; devices with which to call an ambulance or look up the Heimlich maneuver quickly.

Still, technology takes even while it gives, and it's not unreasonable to feel that one of the things it is taking is our ability to stop occasionally, or at least to slow down. We bob along feeling helpless on a frantic current of light and noise, always on the move, our predicament best depicted in the linear leap forwards of the dash. The semicolon represents a way to slow down, to stop,* and to think; it measures time more meditatively than the catchall dash, and it can't be chucked thoughtlessly into just any sentence in place of just any other mark. Even a semicolon that creates a quickness in prose, like the type Rebecca Solnit often uses, requires time and thought to orchestrate. Semicoloned sentences cannot be dashed off.

Back in the city, writing up the lessons he had learned away from "civilization," Thoreau praised a life lived in the present:

---

* A stop without stopping completely. Who wants the full stop right now, with its silence and finality like a red button pressed, or a clock striking midnight?

In any weather, at any hour of the day or night, I have been anxious to improve the nick of time, and notch it on my stick too; to stand on the meeting of two eternities, the past and future, which is precisely the present moment; to toe that line.

As we learn to contend with the technologies of the present moment and look for space in which to feel we, too, are really *present*, not pitched helplessly into the future or anchored to the past, we might find it good to look more often to a much older technology, the semicolon, notched into our sentences; to toe that line.

VIII

PERSUASION AND PRETENSION

Are Semicolons for Snobs?

The claim that the semicolon harbors nefarious ambiguities isn't the only accusation to dog that punctuation mark. People also think semicolons are for highfalutin snobs. Paul Robinson calls them "pretentious." June Casagrande, who writes on language for the *Los Angeles Times,* declares that semicolons are "favored by writers who are so proud they know how to use semicolons that they'll happily shortchange readers to show off their knowledge."

Allegations that the semicolon is pretentious have grown increasingly common in the last few decades, but they date back at least to the late nineteenth century, when one commentator *celebrated* the "elitist" character of the semicolon that so disgusts Robinson and galls Casagrande:

> It seems paradoxical to assert that the simplest method of isolating the masters of modern English literature is carefully to observe the frequency and propriety of their semicolons; and yet, like the Oxford college where the fellows were chosen by the grace with which they were able to dispose of the stones from the plum tart, the semicolon test may prove the final one to determine the author's fitness to rank with august society.

I would no more argue for measuring the intelligence of a person with their use of semicolons than with their ability to finesse plum pits out of tarts; but neither do I hold with obliterating the semicolon, any more than I would refuse to eat a slice of plum tart just because someone somewhere associates them with snobbery. There is no need to hate semicolons without let, or love commas unequivocally: you can react passionately towards individual instances of their usage without having to swear allegiance to, or vendettas against, the marks themselves.

The semicolon has sometimes been associated with elitism, but it certainly doesn't need to be that way. We've already seen Irvine Welsh use it in Scots dialect in the previous chapter, and not because he's trying to make his characters sound like they went to Eton and are internationally ranked in dressage. And a whole host of other writers who venture outside the confines of formal English use semicolons too. They are everywhere in Junot Díaz's *The Brief Wonderous Life of Oscar Wao*, told from the point of view of the title character's friend Yunior in his Dominican-American patois. Charles Chesnutt's "Po' Sandy" captures ex-slave Uncle Julius's speech rhythms with semicolons. It seems to me it's not justifiable either to praise or to punish the semicolon as a snob's mark.

The semicolon has, furthermore, been drafted in the fight for equality. The finest deployment of semicolons I've ever come across, in fact, is in Martin Luther King, Jr.'s "Letter from Birmingham Jail," which

King wrote longhand in the margins of a newspaper while imprisoned in Alabama for civil disobedience. The letter defends King's agitation for civil rights against fellow clergymen who felt he should show more patience. The passage from the letter that contains the remarkable semicolons is a long one, and I suggest reading it out loud to really feel their effects.

Perhaps it is easy for those who have never felt the stinging darts of segregation to say, "Wait." But when you have seen vicious mobs lynch your mothers and fathers at will and drown your sisters and brothers at whim; when you have seen hate filled policemen curse, kick and even kill your black brothers and sisters; when you see the vast majority of your twenty million Negro brothers smothering in an airtight cage of poverty in the midst of an affluent society; when you suddenly find your tongue twisted and your speech stammering as you seek to explain to your six year old daughter why she can't go to the public amusement park that has just been advertised on television, and see tears welling up in her eyes when she is told that Funtown is closed to colored chil-

dren, and see ominous clouds of inferiority beginning to form in her little mental sky, and see
her beginning to distort her personality by de-
veloping an unconscious bitterness toward white
people; when you have to concoct an answer for
a five year old son who is asking: "Daddy, why
do white people treat colored people so mean?";
when you take a cross country drive and find it
necessary to sleep night after night in the uncomfortable corners of your automobile because
no motel will accept you; when you are humili-
ated day in and day out by nagging signs reading "white" and "colored"; when your first name
becomes "nigger," your middle name becomes
"boy" (however old you are) and your last name
becomes "John," and your wife and mother are
never given the respected title "Mrs."; when you
are harried by day and haunted by night by the
fact that you are a Negro, living constantly at
tiptoe stance, never quite knowing what to expect next, and are plagued with inner fears and
outer resentments; when you are forever fighting
a degenerating sense of "nobodiness"—then you
will understand why we find it difficult to wait.

As King was waiting, frustrated, for change, so must the reader wait a full page, held in suspension by those semicolons, while King lists agony after agony, indignity after indignity, before he alights on his final clause, delivered emphatically with an em dash. The experience of reading the sentence is one of waiting breathless and uncomfortable, which amplifies the force of King's description of the misery of waiting for change. This is mimesis at its finest. And this experience of waiting could be created only with the semicolons, which are doing much more here than just separating items in a list or putting some distance between independent clauses. The semicolon is used to open a window on the lived experience of blacks in America in 1963. It's about the furthest thing from an elitist sentiment that I can think of.

Nonetheless, you could say there is certainly something "elite" about this passage, even as it argues for equal rights. Martin Luther King spoke and wrote in a way that lets his work seamlessly slot into Western scholarly tradition and norms. In the rest of the "Letter" and in his writings more generally, he cites the classics of the Western canon—Plato, Aquinas, the Bible, Martin Luther, Abraham Lincoln, Thomas Jefferson, Martin Buber, T. S. Eliot, the Declaration of Independence. His writing is elegant and formal. Although it would be a mistake to chalk up to mere performance King's stylistic choices and his careful cultivation of a distinguished intellectual family tree, it is certainly true that, as a deft rhetorician, King is in full control of the register in which he's writing. The putative audience for his letter, after all, was a group of eight white Southern clergymen. In a sense, everything in the "Letter," from the invocation of St. Augustine to the semicolons, is a coded message that says, "You can take me seriously; I'm *Dr.* King; I know the same things you know."

I'm hardly the first person to home in on the conventionality of King's register. It gets a mention in a speech that the novelist, essayist, and English teacher David Foster Wallace liked to give to black students whose writing he perceived to be, unlike King's, "nonstandard." Wallace gave this speech one-on-one to students he believed would benefit from it. It's long, but here's a taster:

> I don't know whether anybody's told you this or
> not, but when you're in a college English class

you're basically studying a foreign dialect. This dialect is called Standard Written English. . . . In this country, SWE is perceived as the dialect of education and intelligence and power and prestige, and anybody of any race, ethnicity, religion, or gender who wants to succeed in American culture has got to be able to use SWE. This is just How It Is. You can be glad about it or sad about it or deeply pissed off. You can believe it's racist and unfair and decide right here and now to spend every waking minute of your adult life arguing against it, and maybe you should, but I'll tell you something—if you ever want those arguments to get listened to and taken seriously, you're going to have to communicate them in SWE, because SWE is the dialect our nation uses to talk to itself. African-Americans who've become successful and important in US culture know this; that's why King's and X's and Jackson's speeches are in SWE . . . and why black judges and politicians and journalists and doctors and teachers communicate professionally in SWE. . . . And [STUDENT'S NAME], you're going to learn to use it too, because I am going to make you.

This speech, Wallace claims, is in the service of being honest and realistic about the way that language is wrapped up in politics and power. Students should be pressed into choosing to learn what Wallace calls SWE—Standard Written English, or Standard White English, as he acknowledges it might as well be called. The reason students should be required to learn SWE is that they will be at an extreme disadvantage in the world if they do not do so. This is how the world is whether you like it or not, Wallace says, ostensibly congratulating himself on his brave truth telling.

Apparently a few students who were subjected to this speech were offended by it, and one lodged an official complaint with the university. I have some complaints about it, too. Did Wallace pull all his white students into his office for an in-camera chat about how it is that they might be upholding elitist power structures by speaking and writing SWE? Did Wallace call out his colleagues in the academy for failing to find ways to make room for ideas expressed by people who might not know—or might simply choose not to use—the secret-handshake grammar of the powerful? Did he make participation in SWE a choice as fraught with moral and political implications as he made *non*participation in that dialect? No, the onus is on the black student to choose, not on Wallace or anyone else to use his power and privilege to help remake the world.

Later in the essay, he tells the reader that what must have been offensive to the student who complained about his speech was only that he, a privileged white male, was the one making it. Because of his identity, he says, the student just wasn't able to see the "logic" of his speech. Nice try, DFW, but what logic? So—your argument is "We must use one form of speech, Standard Written English, because that's the form of speech we always use." I'm not persuaded that "we are doing this already" is sufficient to justify a claim that "we *ought* to continue to do this" or "we *must* continue to do this." Logic is about uncovering and examining assumptions, not perpetuating them. Maybe there is an intelligent, logical argument to be made for choosing SWE as a shared scholarly and professional dialect— but Wallace didn't bother making it.

What is most infuriating about reading Wallace— more infuriating even than his factual errors and logical hiccups, of which there are many in the "American

Usage" essay*—is that it seems he was equipped to understand, for instance, that language is part of our self-presentation, crucial to our construction and conception of ourselves. He understood better than most people that language, and the choices we make surrounding it, is political, *always*. Yet in his "pep-talk" to black students, he didn't see it as his job to create a world that would be more open to more possible selves than ones like his own. It's a good thing to make students (and even people who've left their student days far behind) aware that there are context-specific costs and benefits in the choice of one English dialect over another. The problem is that Wallace exempts himself (and everyone who already speaks and writes like he

---

* For a taste of some of the problems with Wallace's essay, see the *Language Hat* blog's entry "David Foster Wallace Demolished," http://languagehat.com/david-foster-wallace-demolished/, accessed August 5, 2018. In addition to the mostly sentence-level problems that Language Hat highlights, there are glaring argument-level flaws. Those flaws would require a longish essay to elucidate properly, and this book is not the place. The essay is useful here as an example of a very common and very misguided expectation that users of "standard" English are exempt from justifying that choice.

does) from responsibility for his own choice, by pretending it isn't a choice at all.

It's an attitude in keeping with Wallace's self-proclaimed snobbery. He was profoundly a snob—or as he called it, a SNOOT, an acronym* Wallace's family used for "somebody who knows what dysphemism means and doesn't mind letting you know it." A dysphemism is a derogatory term—like *snoot*, for instance—and you shouldn't feel bad if you didn't know that, nor should you feel exceptionally clever if you did and you got the joke. Each of Wallace's sentences is a stunt of some kind, every clause an Odyssean convolution. For him, being a SNOOT was something to brag about, and it's crucial to his literary style. When I look back on my own snob days, I feel it's something to be embarrassed about. Where Wallace sees moral high ground lush with the fruits of knowledge, I see a desolate valley, in which the pleasures of speaking "properly" and following rules have choked out the very basic ethical principle of giving a shit about what other people have to say.

---

* "Sprachgefühl Necessitates Our Ongoing Tendance."

Wallace cared a lot about language and punctuation, and I have no problem with that. I love that at his book readings, he read his punctuation aloud along with the words, because he put those punctuation marks in his writing for a reason. His enthusiasm for punctuation and for language more broadly is not the problem, and I don't doubt that he took his role as a teacher of young people seriously. What is problematic to me is the direction in which he chose to channel those interests and concerns: he narrowed the conversation about the politics of language rather than expanding it, by making it one-sided and doing what everyone always does—obligating people who aren't participating in the status quo to step it up rather than asking the people enforcing the status quo to think about, and justify, their own standards and values.

So what happens now, if you're ready to entertain the notion that having plum-picking contests and SNOOTing around isn't the most admirable way to behave? What's left, if we aren't supposed to show our respect and love for language by respecting and loving rules?

AGAINST THE RULES?

It'll be clear to you by now that I disagree with the rule mongering of the David Foster Wallace types, and the semicolon hatred of Professor Paul Robinson, the guy who feels "morally compromised" when his pinkie finger plunks the semicolon key. The history of punctuation shows that rules can't be taken for granted as necessary elements of language. For a start, when we consider rules, we have to ask: *whose* rules? Exactly which collection of rules are we supposed to rely upon and remember, when the fortunes of rule systems have depended on their contradicting one another? For over two centuries, grammar books have preached the gospel of rules, and now, when I talk to friends, students, and colleagues about grammar, they lower their voices confidentially to confess sins: *I just don't ever use the semicolon, because I'm afraid I'll do it wrong. I sometimes* want *to use two colons in one sentence, but I'm not* allowed. *I am very confused about the Oxford comma.* Occasionally I've been pulled aside after a talk on the semicolon to be told a story about a dogmatic elementary school English teacher still perched on the now-adult student's shoulder, looking down, judging, even after decades. At times I've felt less like a punctuation theorist than like a punctuation therapist.

Fear, worry, confusion—even if we did manage to agree on one set of rules to follow, we wouldn't be relieved of our anxieties about punctuation. We still have to worry whether we know the rules and have applied them correctly. We have to worry about situations for which we can't find a rule that seems applicable, and hope that the authorities on the *Chicago Manual*'s "Q&A" web page address the oversight immediately. And even if we happen to be very very good at remembering the rules and applying their most obscure precepts, we have to wonder if our assiduous applications of these details will strike the average reader as *mistakes** rather than the markers of precision we hope them to be: if rules are not natural features of language, then they depend upon their being shared knowledge in order to bestow on our writing the clarity and precision they promise. Rules have never in human history—and are not now—freeing us from the pitfalls and challenges of interpreting other people's words and the anxieties of writing down our own.

In spite of this problem, the bromide that *we need to know rules* is constant even among punctuation reformists, and it's such a deeply entrenched idea that

---

* This happens with grammar rules of all kinds, not just punctuation. When I worked at Yale, I rode the Metro North trains from New York to New Haven regularly, and I often stopped at one of the kiosks near the train to get a gin and tonic for the journey. One night, after an especially exhausting conference in the city, I walked up and ordered "two gins and tonic." The person manning the kiosk was briefly speechless at being confronted with such an idiot as myself who couldn't even order properly. Finally, perhaps after considering the possibility I might be too drunk already to serve, she asked me if I meant "two gin and tonics." I opted not to go into the pluralization rule and said, "Sure. The gin is just more important to me than the tonic."

grammar writers rarely (if ever) attempt to justify it. Even the philosopher Theodor Adorno, who wrote a beautiful essay, "Punctuation Marks," which recovered and built upon the humanist ideal of punctuation as musical, advised that rules have to "echo in the background" even in moments where the author "suspends" those rules. Adorno, like just about everyone else writing about punctuation, seems to have believed that we always process writing in terms of its conformity to, or conflict with, rules. When a rule is broken, these theorists believe, we hear the breakage, whether we realize it consciously or not.

But if that were true, it sure would be strange that we can read someone like Shakespeare without having our delicate rule-bound constitutions constantly assaulted by "false syntax," as the early American grammarians called it. Remember those corrections they made to Shakespeare's verse? Perhaps the experience of reading isn't so much a matter of hearing "rules" and "not-rules" as it is about immersing ourselves in a text and adjusting to a way of speaking that might be very foreign to us in terms of time period, culture, or genre. That's a pretty extraordinary skill to have built into our brains, and I'm not sure why we'd *want* to squeeze it out of ourselves by insisting that language is inherently rule-bound.

If rules don't do what they set out to do for us—if rules are just idealizations of language that don't manage either to help us learn to write well, or to describe why a piece of writing is effective or ineffective—does that mean that rules are totally worthless? Not necessarily. In fact, if we can learn to see past rules as the *only* framework with which we can understand and learn to use language, we might be able to see what purposes rules could *really* serve. That is, we can peel away the justification that "rules are *really in* language" and free ourselves to ask instead, "What *good* might rules be, even if they aren't strictly *necessary* or *sufficient*?" Rules, considered as frameworks within which to work rather than as boundaries marking the outer limits of rhetorical possibility, might spur creativity, just as a poet might find it productive to work within the strictures of the sonnet form. But we would be making a big mistake to teach that the only "legal" way to write poetry is to write sonnets. The same goes for punctuation rules.

Perhaps this will be some balm for the souls of some of you who, in spite of the story told in this book, still feel attached to *The Elements of Style* or Fowler or whatever your preferred grammar tome might be. Even if you accept everything I've said in this book about rules, you might still feel, deep down, a love for the idea of grammar rules. But when it comes down to it, I'd wager that the object of your love lies elsewhere. That love is really for the English language, or for orderliness and organization, or for tradition. None of these things is a foolish thing to love. But if we really love English, or if we love the sense of structure that grammar provides, or if we love traditions and a sense of shared linguistic practices across generations, we have to look somewhere else to celebrate that devotion; rules will be, just as they always have been, inadequate to form a protective fence around English. We will never find *the* rules, unshiftable, unchangeable, and incorruptible. There are no such things.

It's worth thinking carefully about the ethical costs of trying to build that fence anyway. A fence keeps things out as surely as it keeps things in. Who is kept out of our conversations, our public life, and our academies by these language-fences? Rules can be an easy, lazy way to put the onus on someone else: if you make a grammar mistake while trying to convey something heartfelt, I can just point out you've used a comma splice and I'm excused from confronting what you were saying, since you didn't say it properly. What if we thought less about rules and more about communication, and considered it our obligation to one another to try to figure out what is really being communicated? Does it truly matter if there's a grammar error in the email from your intern, or on the sandwich board outside the deli that a new immigrant couple has opened, or in a world leader's tweet?* I care a lot more about whether the President's tweets show the values of democracy versus hatred than I do about where he put a comma. During the 2012 elections, when Mitt Romney ran aggressive campaigns misconstruing President Obama's statements on entrepreneurship, Jon Stewart capped off an indictment of Romney's strategy with, "Mr. Romney, hanging your attack on a person's slight

---

* Fuckups can be fun, but it matters who we're laughing at. If you want to, feel free to print a giant poster-size copy of the previous sentence and have a good giggle at this author with multiple degrees ending a sentence with a preposition. But don't be like Bristol's so-called Banksy of punctuation or Acción Ortográfica Quito and go around marking up people's store billboards to correct grammar mistakes. That makes you a vandal and a mean-spirited pedant.

grammatical misstep is what people do in an argument when they're completely fucked and they know they *have* no argument." Indeed. Or it's what they do when they don't want to be bothered to hear the other side in the first place: a grammar attack is quite simply an *ad hominem* attack that looks more legitimate because it's dressed up in a cap and gown.

Those of you readers who speak English as a first language, like I do, enjoy a remarkable privilege: we speak the most widely spoken language in all the world. This is a wonderful advantage for us; the preeminence of English does as much as airplanes and the Internet do to make the world small enough that we can skip across its circumference in ways both real and virtual that our grandparents wouldn't have dreamed possible. At the same time, many native English speakers never experience what it's like to struggle to communicate basic needs to a store clerk; or to be lost on the subway, the air filled with indecipherable phonemes that offer no aid; or to be talked down to as though you're an idiot by someone who has heard your foreign accent. Having lived abroad myself, I can recall with yesterday's clarity the casual callousness of a German pharmacist who pretended for five long minutes that she didn't know I was asking for ibuprofen at the Berlin Hauptbahnhof Apotheke because I said "ich mochte" (I liked) instead of "ich möchte" (I would like); and I can recall with equal clarity the generosity and hospitality of a group of Germans who took the time to have a slow conversation with me in their language while waiting for the TXL bus to come.[*] I know which type of memory I'd rather be in the mind of a tourist, immigrant, Internet forum poster, or any other English-language learner. Having a more advanced knowledge of a language provides a wonderful opportunity to be welcoming and constructive, if you prioritize communication over a set of fictitious rules.

What about that semicolon I argued over with my dissertation adviser so many years ago—the semicolon that launched my deep dive into the history of

---

[*] I lived in Berlin on and off between 2007 and 2013. When I go back to visit now, even though I'm rusty from lack of practice, I find Berliners are *much* keener to speak German with me now that their city has been occupied by hordes of British and American expats, many of whom don't bother to learn a single word of German since they can sail along fine speaking English. Perhaps that's made Berliners look at German learners in a new and more forgiving light.

punctuation and led to this book? Looking back on it now, I was right that it was "legal." Semicolons like the one I deployed are shown in the example sentences for *Chicago Manual of Style* rule 6.54, which treats sentences that use elision. But even though it was legal, it was a bad semicolon. What my adviser, Bob, was reacting to (although he'll fight me on this, I'm sure!) was not a lack of rule-following, but the poor rhythm of the sentence, which his practiced ear detected and rejected. That's the case with so many instances of grammar-rule violations. When your teacher told you that you can't write a one-sentence paragraph, what he or she really meant was "I needed more evidence here" or "This wasn't the right spot in this essay for drama." Great writers use one-sentence paragraphs all the time, but it is true that they don't always work. It might be more efficient to make a rule against writing a one-sentence paragraph than it is to explain why some particular one-sentence paragraph didn't work, but it's misleading.

Even if they aren't the basis by which we read and write, punctuation rules can't just be unthought as though they never existed in the first place. We could not (and perhaps would not *want* to) go back to a time before there were punctuation rules. But maybe we can think *beyond* them now, to develop a new, more functional, more ethical philosophy of punctuation: one that would support a richer way of learning, teaching, using, and loving language. At the very least, by reflecting on the history of the commas, colons, question marks, and semicolons that dot our written language, we can gain some of the perspective necessary to properly evaluate the virtues and vices of rules. After all, it's impossible to confront assumptions that we can't even see.

ACKNOWLEDGMENTS

Although brief in length, this book has been long in the making, and countless people have been essential in bringing it to its final full stop.

Robert J. Richards and Lorraine Daston have been the very best and most generous mentors anyone interested in ideas could have. I'm immensely grateful that they encouraged me to think creatively and to take risks, and for the constancy of their confidence in me.

Long before my graduate school years, Joan Traffas and Sheila Patrick taught me that the past and present are always in conversation with one another.

Adrian Johns at the University of Chicago and Françoise Waquet at the Centre National de Recherche Scientifique in Paris were early advocates for this project, and gamely lent me snippets of their vast expertise in books, language, and the history of the transmission of knowledge. I hope they are reading this book—but not too closely.

The editorial board of Critical Inquiry taught me that what I was really writing about was love and anxiety. Apologies to Jay Williams for all the "French colons" that have probably crept back into the manuscript on its way towards becoming a book.

My agent, Danielle Svetcov, is an absolute dream. In a literary utopia, all the agents would be clones of Danielle. She's worked tirelessly at all hours of the day and night, fearlessly advocated for me and the book, and either calmed or cultivated my ego depending on what it needed day to day.

The team at Ecco, who turned a pile of mere words into this beautiful object, have been magnificent. Denise Oswald, my editor, is the personification of verve. Her energy and sense of humor is evident in every email and every edit. Emma Janaskie patiently taught me the finest distinctions between writing for academics and writing for trade. Along with the production and design team at Ecco, Sara Ridky and Anthony Russo made the book come alive with their gorgeous artwork.

Sundry advice on all manner of things from the aesthetic to the practical was offered generously by Aerin Hyun, Leo Vladimirsky, Benjamin Lorr, Ashley

Wilson, Tim Casey, Peter Trachtenberg, Liz Gately, and Melissa Wachs. My peers in the University of Chicago's Committee on Conceptual and Historical Studies of Science and my colleagues in Bard College's Language and Thinking were the brightest and most generous first audiences for this project that I could have wished for. Jeff Boggs and Lauren Silvers served up Henry James sources and book cover inspiration; the popovers weren't bad either. Isabel Gabel, cofounder of Rage on the Page, got me through afternoons when I really, really did not want to write. Suzanne Daggett, Nadya Ostroff, Leah Holroyd, and Richard Burgess-Dawson kept me distracted while waiting for auction news. Back in 2012, James Harker told me, "You know, there could be a book in that article"; sometimes you were expecting *ein Glas* but you find out that you've unexpectedly gotten *eine große Flasche*. David Elkins solved all my MS Word problems while Christian Blood read my footnotes aloud and chortled gratifyingly. Anurag Dhingra, Christina Bloomquist, and Frankie let me borrow their apartment when I needed somewhere to close myself off and write. Marie Regan offered endless encouragement and advice from afar, and she choreographs one hell of a celebratory dance party over Skype. Anjuli Fatima Raza Kolb is my alchemist, always.

I will always owe more than I can convey to the following people: Jason Emery, who has lent me words when I lacked the right ones, and who has endured my roughest drafts without judgment (once you'd seen the one I concealed in an empty yogurt cup, what was left to hide?); Rachel Ponce, who has spent many hours rescuing little things I lost, like all the footnotes to my dissertation (once) and my sense of self-worth (regularly); Niall Mason, who has expanded the boundaries of my worlds both geographical and intellectual; and finally, John Pharis, Sue Ellen Watson, and Parks Watson, fixed stars who have been there from the very beginning and who deserve their place here at the most important part of any piece of writing:

The End.

NOTES

INTRODUCTION: LOVE, HATE, AND SEMICOLONS

1 "The semicolon has become so hateful": Paul Robinson, "The Philosophy of Punctuation," *The New Republic* (April 26, 1980). Reprinted 2002 at http://www.press.uchicago.edu/Misc/Chicago/721833.html, accessed October 22, 2018.

1 ugliness, or irrelevance: Lynne Truss, *Eats, Shoots and Leaves* (New York: Gotham Press, 2003), p. 108.

1–2 "transvestite hermaphrodites": Kurt Vonnegut, *A Man Without a Country* (New York: Seven Stories Press, 2005).

2 almost 800,000 people: 741.2k shares according to SharedCount.com metrics, using the URLs http://bit.ly/5FNLFV and http://theoatmeal.com/comics/semicolon. Last verified on September 6, 2018.

2 "most feared punctuation mark": "How to Use a Semicolon," The Oatmeal, accessed September 6, 2018. http://theoatmeal.com/comics/semicolon.

2 "pretentious": Robinson, "The Philosophy of Punctuation."

2 downright *trendy*: See Chapter Seven, "Sexy Semicolons."

3 "purely a species of fashion": George Campbell, *The Philosophy of Rhetoric* (London: W. Strahan, 1776), p. 340.

3   "gross mistakes": Robert Lowth, *A Short Introduction to English Grammar: With Critical Notes* (London: A. Millar, 1762), p. xii.

6   "It's tough being a stickler": Truss, *Eats, Shoots and Leaves*, p. 2.

I. DEEP HISTORY: THE BIRTH OF THE SEMICOLON

13   The semicolon was born: On the origins and form of the semicolon, see M. B. Parkes, *Pause and Effect: An Introduction to the History of Punctuation in the West* (Berkeley: University of California Press, 1993), p. 49.

13   The humanists: Paul Grendler, "Humanism," *Oxford Bibliographies* (June 27, 2017), doi: 10.1093/OBO/9780195399301–0002.

14   specially cut: Cambridge University Library, "Pietro Bembo (1470–1547) *De Aetna*," *Manutius and the Bembos* (online exhibition). https://exhibitions.lib.cam.ac.uk/manutius/artifacts/bembo-de-aetna/.

14   sprinkled here and there: Parkes, *Pause and Effect*, p. 49.

17   "ugly, ugly as a tick": Truss, *Eats, Shoots and Leaves*, p. 108.

18   "It is not concealed": Quoted in ibid., p. 48.

II. THE SCIENCE OF SEMICOLONS: AMERICAN GRAMMAR WARS

23   "something like a complete grammar": Goold Brown, *The Grammar of English Grammars* (1851; New York: W. Wood & Co., 1878), p. i.

25   "lay down rules": Lowth, *A Short Introduction to English Grammar*, p. xiii.

27   "few precise rules": Ibid., p. 169.

27 analogous to the rests: Ibid., p. 172.

27 *English Grammar* was a blockbuster success: John A. Nietz, "Old Secondary School Grammar Textbooks," *English Journal* 54, no.6 (September 1965): 541–546, http://www.jstor.org/stable/811408.

27 "the best-selling producer": Charles Monaghan, preface to *The Murrays of Murray Hill* (Brooklyn, NY: Urban History Press, 1998), p. vii. Italics mine.

28 at least *one hundred and ten*: Alma Blount, *An English grammar, for use in high and normal schools and colleges* (New York: H. Holt, 1914), p. 336.

28 a new system of parsing verbs: F. A. Barbour, "The History of English Grammar Teaching," *Educational Review* 12 (1896): 492.

28 extending his predecessors' criticisms: Ibid., p. 497.

29 "veer his course": Brown, *Grammar of English Grammars*, p. 50.

29 when Kirkham revised: Ibid., p. 51.

29 "filled with glad wonder": Ibid., p. 46.

30 In one particularly efficient passage: Ibid., p. 52.

31 more boasting: Kirkham in the *Knickerbocker*, quoted in ibid., p. 50.

31 Brown bit back: Ibid.

32 protests from parents . . . and school officials: See, for instance, the objections of parents in A. M. Leonard, "The Teaching of Grammar: Meeting at the Educational Room," *Massachusetts Teacher and Journal of Home and School Education* (July 1, 1867): 243, and also the State of Connecticut's rejection of grammar recounted in Barbour, "History of English Grammar Teaching," p. 500.

32 as early as 1827: "Philosophical Essays 8," *Masonic Mirror and Mechanics' Intelligencer* (February 24, 1827): 66.

32 came to a boil by 1850: Barbour, "History of English Grammar Teaching," p. 498.

32 persisted through the rest of the nineteenth century: See ibid., 500; and Charles H. Watson, "Shifts in Educational Methods," *The Watchman* (May 10, 1900): 14.

34 "laws of language": I. J. Morris, preface to *Morris's grammar. A philosophical and practical grammar of the English language, dialogically and progressively arranged; in which every word is parsed according to its use* (New York: T. Holman, 1858), p. iii.

34 "errors" and "absurdities": Ibid., vi–xv.

34 eviscerating the stale precepts: Ibid.

34 "If the truth be disagreeable": Ibid.

36 virtues of the natural sciences: G. Dallas Lind, "Natural Science in Common Schools," *Massachusetts Teacher* (August 1, 1873): 274. Another critic argued that grammar was important as a science, but that only prior study in natural science would enable students subsequently to investigate the fundamentals of English: physics as a prerequisite for language rules, as it were. See C.A.C., "The Natural and Physical Sciences in Our Grammar and High Schools: A paper read before the Middlesex County Teachers' Association by C. A. Cole," *Massachusetts Teacher* (June 1, 1874): 244.

37 a system of diagrams: Stephen W. Clark, preface to *A practical grammar: in which words, phrases, and sentences are classified according to their offices, and their relation to each other: illustrated by a complete set of diagrams* (New York: A. S. Barnes, 1847), p. iv.

37 thought of them that way: See Roberto Torretti, "Nineteenth Century Geometry," in *The Stanford Encyclopedia of Philosophy*, ed. Edward N. Zalta, plato.stanford.edu/archives/sum2010/entries/geometry-19th/; and Jerome Fellmann,

Arthur Getis, and Judith Getis, *Human Geography: Landscapes of Human Activities* (Madison, WI, 1997), p. 3.

37 believed the two disciplines were essential: See "Subjects and Means of Instruction," *American Journal of Education* 10 (March 1861): 141.

37 "perfect" and "useful": Anon., "Teachers and Teachers' Seminaries," *American Annals of Education* 7 (February 1837): 49.

39 "leading principles, definitions, and rules": Peter Bullions, *The Principles of English Grammar; comprising the substance of the most approved English grammars extant; with copious exercises in parsing and syntax; a new edition, revised, re-arranged and improved for the use of schools* (New York: Pratt, Oakley, 1859), p. viii.

39 "in larger type": Ibid.

39 "to convey to the reader": Ibid., p. 151.

39 "the duration of the pauses": Ibid., p. 152.

39 "The foregoing rules": Ibid., p. 155.

42 "Some may begin to think": Brown, *Grammar of English Grammars*, p. 22.

III. SEXY SEMICOLONS

45 "Forty-three wore the moustache": "Beards, Smooth Faces, and So On," *Chicago Daily Tribune*, March 16, 1857, p. 2.

46 the *un*fashionableness of two other marks: Brown, *Grammar of English Grammars*, p. 773.

46 "the parenthesis is now": T. Churchill, *A New Grammar of the English Language* (London: W. Simpkin and R. Marshall, 1823), p. 362. Quoted in Brown, *Grammar of English Grammars*, p. 773.

46 "nearly obsolete": Rufus Nutting, *A practical grammar*

of the English language: accompanied with notes, critical and explanatory (Montpelier, VT: E. P. Walton, 1826), p. 126; and Bradford Frazee, *An improved grammar of the English language, on the inductive system, etc.* (Philadelphia, 1844), p. 187. Both quoted in Brown, *Grammar of English Grammars*, p. 773.

46 "little moons": Parkes, *Pause and Effect*, p. 215.

47 "The COLON is now so seldom used": Oliver C. Felton, *A concise manual of English grammar: arranged on the principle of analysis: containing the first principles and rules, fully illustrated by examples . . . and a series of parsing lessons in regular gradation from the simplest to the most abstruse* (Salem, MA: W. & S. B. Ives, 1843), p. 140. Quoted in Brown, *Grammar of English Grammars*, p. 773.

47 "we should not let children use them": "Punctuation III," *The Common School Journal* (February 1, 1850): 42.

47 "But who cannot perceive": Brown, *Grammar of English Grammars*, p. 773.

47 "once very fashionable": Ibid.

48 "The use of the semicolon": H. W. Fowler, *A Dictionary of Modern English Usage* (1926; Hertfordshire: Wordsworth Editions, 1994), p. 568.

49 midcentury grammarians waffled: Brown, *Grammar of English Grammars*, pp. 770–771. Brown gives a detailed account of the various opinions on punctuation's classification.

50 four possibilities: G. P. Quackenbos, *An English Grammar* (New York: D. Appleton, 1863), p. 264.

50 perfectly acceptable to link together: See, for instance, Brown's *Grammar of English Grammars*, p. 771: "Of the different kinds of verse, or 'the structure of Poetical Composition,' some of the old prosodists took little or no notice, because they thought it their chief business, to treat of syllables, and determine the orthoëpy of words."

51 grammarians distinguished between rhetorical pauses: See William Chauncey Fowler, *English Grammar* (New York, 1881), p. 743.

52 still permissible: Ibid., p. 749.

52 They generally prescribed them: See F. A. White, *English Grammar* (London, 1882), p. 212.

52 "but one use of the semicolon": California State Board of Education, *English Grammar* (Sacramento, CA, 1881), p. 265.

53 "Where is the man": John Van Ness Standish, "Too Much Teaching by Rote," *Chicago Daily Tribune*, December 24, 1899.

53 "From childhood's earliest hour": "Power of Points: Punctuation That Upset Work of Solons," *Boston Daily Globe*, January 20, 1901, p. 29.

54 "made trouble in the laws": From *The Indianapolis Journal*, "A semicolon Before a Supreme Court: A Legal Treatise on Punctuation or a Changed Method Needed," *New York Times*, December 31, 1895.

55 The Massachusetts Supreme Court had issued: David Cushing & another v. Paul B. Worrick, [no number in original], 75 Mass. 382; 1857 Mass. LEXIS 356; 9 Gray 382.

IV. LOOSE WOMEN AND LIQUOR LAWS: THE SEMICOLON WREAKS HAVOC IN BOSTON

57 "It was an unimportant": "Saloons Shut by Semicolon," *Chicago Daily Tribune*, December 16, 1900, p. 50.

58 "The lawyer brushed the dust off": Ibid.

58 "That no sale of spirituous or intoxicating liquor": Ibid.

59 "was meant to be and should be construed": Ibid.

60 the barman's attorney insisted: "A Semicolon," *Boston Daily Globe*, December 6, 1900, p. 5.

60 "seemed to take a good bit of enjoyment": Ibid.

61 "throw light": Commonwealth v. George H. Kelley; Same v. James Sutcliffe, [no number in original], 177 Mass. 221; 1900 Mass. LEXIS 1038.

61 "punctuation may be disregarded": Cushing v. Worrick, 9 Gray 382, paraphrased in ibid.

61–62 "The cause of all the trouble": "Power of Points," p. 29.

62 "Marks of punctuation may not control": Quoted in ibid.

63 Police were ordered: "Saloons Shut by Semicolon," p. 50.

63 "the proposition before the senate": "Semicolon Stays," *Boston Daily Globe*, April 11, 1901, p. 1.

64 "well known throughout the country": Willard Holcomb, "Latter-Day Puritans: Boston Not Entirely Devoid of Alcoholic Glee," *Washington Post*, June 2, 1901, p. 19.

66 "the greatest provoker of profanity": Ibid.

66 "If every member of this house": "Semicolon Law Stays on Books," *Boston Daily Globe*, April 7, 1904, p. 1.

67 "friends and foes of the semicolon": "Liquor Hours: Closing and Present Law Considered," *Boston Daily Globe*, February 8, 1905, p. 4.

68 put to a popular vote: "Plain, Common Sense," *Boston Daily Globe*, November 28, 1906, p. 6.

68 The people of Massachusetts approved: "Hotel Owners Getting in Line," *Boston Daily Globe*, December 13, 1906, p. 6.

69 "good sense": Ibid.

69 "At last": "Revelry in Boston,: The Gorgonian Glare of Boston Virtue as Cure for the Drink Habit," *New York Sun*. Reprinted in *Boston Daily Globe*, January 15, 1907, p. 10.

70 "members of the association": "Hotel Men at Banquet Board," *Boston Daily Globe*, February 8, 1905, p. 4.

V. THE MINUTIAE OF MERCY

73 "The modern Court": Larry M. Eig et al., *Statutory Construction and Interpretation: General principles and recent trends, statutory structure and legislative drafting conventions, drafting federal grant statutes, and tracking current federal legislation and regulations* (Alexandria, VA: TheCapital.Net, 2010), p. 11.

73 "true meaning": United States Nat'l Bank of Oregon v. Independent Ins. Agents, 508 U.S. 439 (1993) at 454. Quoted in Eig et. al., *Statutory Construction*, p. 11.

73 "the Court remains reluctant": Eig et. al., *Statutory Construction*, p. 11.

74 "punctuation is no part of a statute": Hammock v. Loan and Trust Co., 105 U.S. 77 (1881) at 84–85.

74 "punctuation is the most fallible": Ewing v. Burnet, 36 U.S. 41 (1835).

74 "punctuation is no part of the English language": Holmes v. Phoenix Ins. Co., 9S F. 240. Quoted in Feliciano v. Aquino, GR No. L-10201 (1957).

75 a woman gets out of a parking ticket: Sarah Larimer, "Ohio Appeals Court Ruling Is a Victory for Punctuation, Sanity," *Washington Post*, July 1, 2015, accessed September 9, 2018, https://www.washingtonpost.com/news/post-nation/wp/2015/07/01/ohio-appeals-court-ruling-is-a-victory-for-punctuation-sanity/?noredirect=on&utm_term=.e5a5a0c0dd89.

76 "semi-colon which the appellant views": Feliciano v. Aquino, GR No. L-10201 (1957).

76 "We find the defendant": State v. Merra, 103 N.J.L. 361 (1927).

77 Alexander Simpson argued: "Semicolon Plea Fails to Save Murderer," *New York Times*, May 17, 1927, p. 24.

77 In his dissenting opinion: State v. Merra, 103 N.J.L. 361 (1927).

79 "It does not appear": Ibid.

79 finally making its way to the summer residence: "Hope Fading for Convicted Slayer," *Boston Daily Globe*, August 2, 1927, p. 5.

80 Merra went to the electric chair: "Merra Is Executed; Says 'I Die Innocent,'" *New York Times*, August 6, 1927, p. 28.

80 "unusually large": "Bridegroom Is Executed 80 Hours After Wedding," *The Atlanta Constitution*, August 6, 1927, p. 18.

84 "What more can two immigrants from Italy expect?": Eric Foner, "Sacco and Vanzetti," *The Nation* (August 20, 1977): 137.

84 anti-Irish sentiments: W. H. A. Williams, *'Twas Only an Irishman's Dream: The Image of Ireland and the Irish in American Popular Song Lyrics, 1800–1920* (Urbana: University of Illinois Press, 1996), p. 148.

VI. CARVING SEMICOLONS IN STONE

91–92 "Rules and regulations": *Manual of style, being a compilation of the typographical rules in force at the University of Chicago press, to which are appended specimens of types in use* (Chicago: University of Chicago Press, 1906), p. v.

92 nineteen regulations: Ibid.

93 "what everybody else calls it": *The Chicago Manual of Style: For Authors, Editors, and Copywriters* (Chicago: University of Chicago Press, 1982), p. vii.

93 "much more a 'how-to' book": Ibid.

93 "the subjective element": Ibid., p. 132.

93 "recommend a single rule": Russell David Harper, preface to *The Chicago Manual of Style*, 16th ed. (Chicago: University of Chicago Press, 2010).

94 "extrapolate": "Numbers," *The Chicago Manual of Style Online*, accessed September 4, 2018, https://www.chicago manualofstyle.org/qanda/data/faq/topics/Numbers/faq0008 .html. See also "Citation, Documentation of Sources," *The Chicago Manual of Style Online*, accessed September 4, 2018, https://www.chicagomanualofstyle.org/qanda/data/faq/topics/ Documentation/faq0028.html.

94 "logical application": *The Chicago Manual of Style*, 17th ed. (Chicago: University of Chicago Press, 2017), p. 364.

94 Turkish and Arabic: Harun Küçük, reply to the author's Facebook post, September 16, 2017.

95 "the California stop": Paul Festa, Skype call with the author, February 18, 2018.

95 "in Texas": Tim Casey, reply to the author's Facebook post, September 16, 2017.

VII. SEMICOLON SAVANTS

97 a "golly" or two: Mark Twain, *Mark Twain's Library of Humor*, ed. Washington Irving (New York: Random House, 2010), p. 175.

97 "The damned half-developed foetus": Shaun Usher, *Letters of Note* (Edinburgh: Canongate Unbound, 2013), p. 206.

98 "printer's proof-reader was improving": Mark Twain, *Autobiography of Mark Twain, Volume 1: The Complete and Authoritative Edition*, ed. Harriet E. Smith, Benjamin Griffin, Victor Fischer, and Michael Barry Frank (Oakland: University of California Press, 2010), p. 677.

104 "I use [the semicolon]": John Henley, "The End of the Line?" *The Guardian*, April 3, 2008, accessed September 4, 2018, https://www.theguardian.com/world/2008/apr/04/france.britishidentity.

105 "Coleridge has chosen": Irving N. Rothman, "Coleridge on the Semi-colon in *Robinson Crusoe*: Problems in Editing Defoe," *Studies in the Novel* 27, no. 3 (1995): 320–340, http://www.jstor.org/stable/29533073.

106 "I shaved and showered": Raymond Chandler, *The Big Sleep, Farewell, My Lovely, The High Window* (New York: A. A. Knopf, 2002), p. 137.

108 "would you convey my compliments": Usher, *Letters of Note*, p. 78.

108 Chandler responded with a poem: Shaun Usher, "God damn it, I split it so it will stay split," *Letters of Note* (blog), April 20, 2012, http://www.lettersofnote.com/2012/04/god-damn-it-i-split-it-so-it-will-stay.html.

110 "If you can go past": Raymond Chandler, "Oscar Night in Hollywood," *The Atlantic* (March 1948), https://www.theatlantic.com/magazine/archive/1948/03/oscar-night-in-hollywood/305705/.

114 "I didn't mind what she called me": Raymond Chandler, *The Big Sleep* (1939; New York: Vintage Books, 1992), p. 158.

116 "weak-charactered writers": Truss, *Eats, Shoots and Leaves*, p. 126.

118 "The sweat wis lashing": Irvine Welsh, *Trainspotting* (New York: W. W. Norton, 1996), p. 3.

119 "It wis good fir a while": Irvine Welsh, "A Soft Touch," *The Acid House* (New York: W. W. Norton, 1995); reprinted in Dohra Ahmad, *Rotten English: A Literary Anthology* (New York: W. W. Norton, 2007), p. 267.

120 "That bygone time": Rebecca Solnit, "Diary," *London Review of Books* 35, no. 16 (2013): 32–33, https://www.lrb.co.uk/v35/n16/rebecca-solnit/diary.

121 "American Men commit murder-suicides": Rebecca Solnit, *Men Explain Things to Me* (New York: Haymarket Books, 2014), p. 24.

121 "women are capable": Ibid, p. 35.

122 "Good things came about": Solnit, "Diary."

123 a dramatic chase scene: "Islands," *Planet Earth II*, BBC Natural History Unit, BBC America, and Zweites Deutsches Fernsehen, February 18, 2017.

124 three and a half years: Emily Badiozzaman, "27 Mind-Blowing Facts About the Making of *Planet Earth II*," *ShortList* (blog), December 12, 2016, https://www.shortlist.com/entertainment/tv/making-of-planet-earth-ii-david-attenborough-how-they-made/71586.

124 "Remember that writing is not typing": Rebecca Solnit, "How to Be a Writer," *Literary Hub* (blog), September 13, 2016, https://lithub.com/how-to-be-a-writer-10-tips-from-rebecca-solnit/.

125 there were still first-run copies: Philip Hoare, "What *Moby-Dick* Means to Me," *New Yorker* (November 3, 2011), https://www.newyorker.com/books/page-turner/what-moby-dick-means-to-me.

126 "But if there are any of our readers": "Book Notices," *United States Democratic Review* (Langtree and O'Sullivan, 1852), vol. 30, p. 93.

126 "The style of his tale": Quoted in Hershel Parker, *Herman Melville: A Biography* (Baltimore: Johns Hopkins University Press, 1996), p. 18.

127 "And, as for me": Herman Melville, *Moby-Dick: or, The*

Whale (1851; New York: Charles Scribner's Sons, 1902), p. 96.

128 "Finally: It was stated": Ibid., p. 123.

128 "'Moby-Dick' is not a novel": Hoare, "What *Moby-Dick* Means to Me."

129 "The plot is meagre": *London Britannia*, November 8, 1851.

130 "When instantly, the entire ship careens": Melville, *Moby-Dick*, p. 264.

131 "In the case of a small Sperm Whale": Ibid., p. 261.

132 "Its oceanic reach": Hoare, "What *Moby-Dick* Means to Me."

133 "Is it that by its indefiniteness": Melville, *Moby-Dick*, p. 169.

134 "mystical and well nigh ineffable": Ibid., p. 162.

134 "horror": Ibid.

134 "almost despair[ed]": Ibid.

135 "Mr. Melville grows wilder": Review in *New York Evangelist*, November 20, 1851. Quoted in *Herman Melville: The Contemporary Reviews*, ed. Hershel Parker and Brian Higgins (Cambridge: Cambridge University Press, 2009), p. 379.

137 "there is something really overwhelming": D. H. Lawrence, *Studies in Classic American Literature* (1923; New York: Cambridge University Press, 2003), vol. 2, p. 142.

137 "acute periodic exasperation": Edward Jenks, *The Independent Review* (T. F. Unwin, 1905), vol. 6, p. 105.

138 "cumbrous and difficult": Ibid., p. 109.

138 "a more difficult book": William Thomas Stead, *The Review of Reviews* (Office of the Review of Reviews, 1905), p. 314.

138 "unreadable": Ibid., p. 315.

138 "Life is too short": Ibid.

138 "the seasoned reader": *The Reader Magazine* (Indianapolis: Bobbs-Merrill, 1905), vol. 5, p. 381.

139 "Someone has said": "William James," *The Chautauquan: A Weekly Newsmagazine* (May 1908).

140 becomes tortured and effortful: For the comparison of these two passages, see Royal A. Gettmann, "Henry James's Revision of *The American*," *American Literature* 16, no. 4 (1945): 289, doi:10.2307/2920715.

142 "He glared at her a moment": Henry James, *The Portrait of a Lady* (London: Macmillan & Co., 1881), p. 247.

142 "His kiss was like white lightning": Henry James, *The Portrait of a Lady* (1908; Hertfordshire: Wordsworth Editions, 1999), p. 499.

143 In the revised version: Dominic J. Bazzanella, "The Conclusion to *The Portrait of a Lady* Re-examined," *American Literature* 41, no. 1 (1969): 55–63, doi:10.2307/2924346. As Bazzanella and others point out, partly this was the fault of reviewers of the 1881 edition, who couldn't accept the ambiguity of James's original ending. Still, James *chose* to bend to those criticisms.

144 "the reinstatement of the vague": William James, *The Principles of Psychology* (1890; New York: Dover, 1950), p. 254.

145 "The boundary line of the mental": Ibid., p. 6.

145 "Use the word 'field'": William James, *Manuscript Lectures*, ed. Frederick Burkhardt and Fredson Bowers (Cambridge, MA: Harvard University Press, 1988), p. 220.

145 He used "vague" as a compliment: James, *Principles*, p. 186.

145 "used to gloss over": Robinson, "Philosophy of Punctuation."

147 "exotic" and "transcends the limits": Hans-Johann Glock,

"Was Wittgenstein an Analytic Philosopher?" *Metaphilosophy* 35 (July 2004): 419.

147 "Der Philosoph behandelt": Ludwig Wittgenstein, *Philosophische Untersuchungen* (Oxford: Basil Blackwell, 1958), p. 91.

148 "The philosopher's treatment": Ludwig Wittgenstein, *Philosophical Investigations*, 2nd ed., trans. G. E. M. Anscombe (Oxford: Basil Blackwell, 1968), p. 255.

148 "profound" semicolon: Erich Heller, *The Importance of Nietzsche* (Chicago: University of Chicago Press, 1988), p. 142.

149 "As a rule": [Unsigned review], *Blackwood's Magazine* 131 (March 1882): 374–382; reprinted in Roger Gard, *Henry James* (New York: Routledge, 2013), p. 103.

151 James's very first interview: Preston Lockwood, "Henry James's First Interview," *New York Times*, March 21, 1915.

153 Heinrich von Kleist used the dash: *"Er stieß noch dem letzten viehischen Mordknecht, der ihren schlanken Leib umfaßt hielt, mit dem Griff des Degens ins Gesicht, daß er, mit aus dem Mund vorquellendem Blut, zurücktaumelte; bot dann der Dame, unter einer verbindlichen, französischen Anrede den Arm, und führte sie, die von allen solchen Auftritten sprachlos war, in den anderen, von der Flamme noch nicht ergriffenen, Flügel des Palastes, wo sie auch völlig bewußtlos niedersank. Hier—traf er, da bald darauf ihre erschrockenen Frauen erschienen, Anstalten, einen Arzt zu rufen; versicherte, indem er sich den Hut aufsetzte, daß sie sich bald erholen würde; und kehrte in den Kampf zurück."* See Heinrich von Kleist, "Die Marquise von O . . . ," http://gutenberg.spiegel.de/buch/die-marquise-von-o-1–580/1.

153 "the dashtard": James Marcus, reply to the author's Facebook post, September 16, 2017.

154 "live deep": Henry David Thoreau, *Walden* (1854; New York: Thomas Y. Crowell, 1910), p. 118.

156 "In any weather": Ibid., pp. 19–20.

VIII. PERSUASION AND PRETENSION: ARE SEMICOLONS FOR SNOBS?

159 "pretentious": Robinson, "Philosophy of Punctuation."

159 "favored by writers": June Casagrande, "A Word, Please: Writers Who Use Semicolons Aren't Thinking About the Reader," *Los Angeles Times*, July 23, 2015, http://www.latimes.com/tn-hbi-et-0723-casagrande-20150723-story.html.

160 "It seems paradoxical": E. H. Mullin, "A Plea for the Semicolon," *The Chap-Book* (February 1, 1898), p. 247.

162 "Perhaps it is easy": Martin Luther King, "Letter from Birmingham Jail," www.stanford.edu/group/King/frequentdocs/birmingham.pdf.

165 "I don't know": David Foster Wallace, *Consider the Lobster* (New York: Little, Brown, 2006), Kindle location 1410.

168 what must have been offensive: Ibid., Kindle location 1542.

170 a SNOOT: Ibid., Kindle location 922.

171 he read his punctuation aloud: Andrew Adam Newman, "How Should a Book Sound? And What About Footnotes?" *New York Times*, January 20, 2006, p. E33.

CONCLUSION: AGAINST THE RULES?

176 "echo in the background": Theodor W. Adorno, "Punctuation Marks," trans. Shierry Weber Nicholsen, *Antioch Review* 48 (Summer 1990): 305.

179 "Mr. Romney": Carol Hartsell, "Jon Stewart Slams You-Didn't-Build-That-Gate in Romney, Fox News' Face," *HuffPost*, July 26, 2012, https://www.huffingtonpost.com/2012/07/26/jon-stewart-you-didnt-build-that_n_1705264.html. Italics mine.

INDEX

ABOUT THE AUTHOR

Cecelia Watson is a historian and philosopher of science, and a teacher of writing and the humanities. She is currently on Bard College's faculty in Language and Thinking. Previously she was an American Council of Learned Societies New Faculty Fellow at Yale University, where she was also a fellow of the Whitney Humanities Center and was jointly appointed in the humanities and philosophy departments. Prior to that she was a research fellow at the Max Planck Institute for the History of Science in Berlin, Germany, where she also served as scientific advisor, curator, and moderator for the Haus der Kulturen der Welt, a public center for contemporary arts and culture.